T0083174

# The Oxford Book of Descants

## *Melody edition*

*Edited by* Julian Elloway

MUSIC DEPARTMENT

OXFORD
UNIVERSITY PRESS

OXFORD
UNIVERSITY PRESS

Great Clarendon Street, Oxford OX2 6DP,
United Kingdom

Oxford University Press is a department of the University of Oxford.
It furthers the University's objective of excellence in research, scholarship,
and education by publishing worldwide. Oxford is a registered trade mark of
Oxford University Press in the UK and in certain other countries

This collection © Oxford University Press 2012

Each composer has asserted their right under the Copyright, Designs
and Patents Act, 1988, to be identified as the Composer of their Work(s)

Julian Elloway has asserted his right under the Copyright, Designs
and Patents Act, 1988, to be identified as the Editor of this Work

First published 2012

All rights reserved. No part of this publication may be reproduced,
stored in a retrieval system, or transmitted, in any form or by any means,
without the prior permission in writing of Oxford University Press

Permission to perform this work in public
(except in the course of divine worship) should normally be obtained from
a local performing right licensing organization, unless the owner or the occupier
of the premises being used already holds a licence from such an organization.
Likewise, permission to make and exploit a recording of these works
should be obtained from a local mechanical copyright licensing organization

Enquiries concerning reproduction outside the scope of the above
should be directed to the Music Rights Department, Oxford University Press,
at music.permissions.uk@oup.com or at the address above

ISBN 978–0–19–338680–8

Music origination by Julian Elloway
Printed in Great Britain on acid-free paper by
Caligraving Ltd, Thetford, Norfolk.

Every effort has been made to seek permission for the use of all
copyright items in this book. In the event that any item has been
overlooked, the publishers will be glad to rectify this on reprint.

# PREFACE

Although the hymn descant may be traced from the Renaissance practice of fauxbourdon, where the cantus firmus, or plainchant melody, appeared in the tenor below one or more upper parts, the modern practice of putting an extra line above a tune already in the top part appears to date from the early twentieth century. Notable early publications include Athelstan Riley's 1916 *A Collection of Faux-Bourdons and Descants for the French Ecclesiastical Melodies and other Tunes in the English Hymnal* (the earliest printed collection with 'Descant' in its title, as far as I am aware) and Alan Gray's 1920 *A Book of Descants* (Gray was for 37 years organist of Trinity College, Cambridge, the first of a distinguished list of Cambridge descant composers). Among hymn books, *Songs of Praise* (1925 and 1931) included a number of descant and fauxbourdon settings and, in 1950, *Hymns Ancient & Modern Revised* included descants (many by Sydney H Nicholson), alongside the fauxbourdon settings of earlier editions. At King's College, Cambridge, the carol arrangements of David Willcocks and his successors, recorded and broadcast in carol services, have broadened the popularity of the descant. Sir David's distinguished contribution, starting with the descants included in the original 1961 *Carols for Choirs*, continues to the present day, and I am delighted to have been able to include some of the more recent of these.

This collection includes a range of descants from those of Gray and Nicholson, Edward Bairstow, William Harris, and Harold Darke, right through to the twenty-first century with many newly commissioned items. In between there is a selection from a wide variety of sources, some long established and others recently published. Overall, the preference is for descants that draw attention to the words and not to themselves, that are sensitive to the words with which they are most frequently sung, and that are written with sympathy to the idiom of the original hymn melody (sometimes by the composer of the original hymn). That said, there are also a few striking examples whose effect is partly caused by their notably different harmonic idiom.

Some descants work well for choral festivals and services where the choir is the focus of attention, and others are particularly appropriate for broadcast services where the effect is heard by a non-singing audience. However, the descants selected for this collection are intended for ordinary use in worship where, although sung by and enjoyed by the choir, they are to be appreciated by the congregation, enhancing the meaning of the words and intensifying the sung prayer of the worshipper. This is a heavy responsibility for those choosing descants. It also means that they should be rehearsed, be sung well, and be considered no less important than every other part of the service. Less is more: there is no need automatically to sing a descant to a hymn just because the descant is known. The fewer descants in a service, the more special and important is each; it is better to allow every one to be significant and telling.

Although the texts that are shown here with the music are mostly final verses, descants need not always be sung to the last verse. Nor need they invariably be sung fortissimo throughout. They are part of a wider repertoire for providing variety and illuminating the words that includes unison verses (tutti, or upper voices or lower voices—with or without alternative harmonies), verses that are unaccompanied after the opening bars, or verses that are accompanied by different combinations of instruments or organ without pedals. Some descants are effective if tenors also sing the descant an octave lower. Many of the best descants are written specifically for, and indeed only 'work' for, one set of words and not for others to which the same tune may be sung. In two cases we have given the same tune twice, with different words and different descants for each.

Descants generally work best with a melody that has a strong bass line, preferably played on an organ with an independent pedal section. This means that folk tunes, Taizé chants, etc. are often unsuitable for a descant. Similarly, many recent worship songs require a more flexible approach from the choir and instrumentalists that is outside the scope of this anthology; however, this collection does include a number of folk melodies and worship songs that lend themselves to a conventional descant treatment.

The descants in this volume are mostly unison, but with occasional extra parts, especially in final bars. A second key is presented where both keys are widely used and the descant range is still accessible in the higher key. Some descants work with SATB harmonies that may have been used in previous verses, and others with altered harmonies in the specially written organ part, as indicated in the music.

The decision to include a small number of descants that many choir singers know and may already own is justified by the convenience of having these descants within a single volume. Of course, singers will not find all their personal favourites here, but the hope must be that many of the descants included in this volume will soon be added to the list of favourites.

I am grateful to many friends and colleagues who have shared their expertise and experience, in particular from Oxford University Press, the Royal School of Church Music, and the Diocese of Gloucester, to others who have offered valuable suggestions and advice, and to choirs and congregations that have tested the descants in worship.

JULIAN ELLOWAY
*Stroud, 2012*

# CONTENTS


| TUNE | DESCANT COMPOSER | NO. | PAGE |
|---|---|---|---|
| ABBOT'S LEIGH (in C and D) | Antony Baldwin | 1 | 2, 3 |
| ABERYSTWYTH | Alan Gray | 2 | 4 |
| ABRIDGE (in D and C) | Christopher Gower | 3 | 4 |
| ADESTE, FIDELES | David Willcocks | 4 | 5 |
| ALLELUIA No. 1 | Anthony F Carver and Donald Davison | 5 | 5 |
| ANGEL VOICES (in D and C) | John Cooke | 6 | 6 |
| ANGELS' SONG | Donald Davison | 89 | 54 |
| ANIMA CHRISTI (in F and G) | David Willcocks | 7 | 6, 7 |
| AURELIA | Adrian Lucas | 8 | 7 |
| AUS DER TIEFE | James Vivian | 9 | 8 |
| AUSTRIA (in E♭ and F) | Thomas H Ingham | 10 | 8 |
| BEAUTY FOR BROKENNESS | Ashley Grote | 11 | 9 |
| BETHLEHEM (in F and G) | David Willcocks | 56 | 37 |
| BLAENWERN (in G and F) | John Scott | 12 | 10 |
| CARLISLE (in E♭ and D) | Sydney H Nicholson | 13 | 11 |
| COE FEN | Kenneth Naylor | 14 | 11 |
| CORVEDALE | Maurice Bevan | 15 | 12 |
| CRIMOND | Donald Davison | 16 | 12 |
| CROSS OF JESUS (in G and F) | Paul Leddington Wright | 17 | 12, 13 |
| CRUCIFER (in D and C) | Harold Darke | 18 | 13 |
| CWM RHONDDA | John Scott | 19 | 14 |
| DARWALL'S 148th (in D and C) | Sydney H Nicholson | 20 | 14, 15 |
| DEUS TUORUM MILITUM (in C and B♭) | Simon Lole | 21 | 15 |
| DIX (in A♭ and G) | John Wilson | 22 | 16 |
| DOMINUS REGIT ME (in G and F) | Sydney H Nicholson | 23 | 16, 17 |
| DOWN AMPNEY | David Willcocks | 24 | 17 |
| DUKE STREET | Philip Moore | 25 | 17 |
| EASTER HYMN | John Rutter | 26 | 18 |
| EISENACH | Harrison Oxley | 27 | 18 |
| ENGLEBERG (in F and G) | David Willcocks | 28 | 19 |
| EVENTIDE | David Willcocks | 29 | 20 |
| FAITHFUL ONE | David Thorne | 30 | 20 |
| FAITHFULNESS (in E♭ and D) | Paul Leddington Wright and Robert Prizeman | 31 | 21 |
| FATHER, WE ADORE YOU | William Llewellyn | 32 | 21 |
| FATHER, WE LOVE YOU | William Llewellyn | 33 | 22 |
| FOREST GREEN | Thomas Armstrong | 34 | 22 |
| GERONTIUS (in A♭ and G) | Robert Gower | 35 | 23 |
| GOD OF THE POOR | Ashley Grote | 11 | 9 |
| GOD REST YOU MERRY | Christopher Robinson | 36 | 23 |
| GUITING POWER | John Barnard | 37 | 24 |
| HANOVER | Alan Gray | 38 | 24 |
| HEINLEIN | James Vivian | 9 | 8 |
| HELMSLEY | John Rutter | 39 | 25 |
| HIGHWOOD | Robert Gower | 40 | 25 |
| HOLY IS THE LORD (in A and G) | Ashley Grote | 41 | 26 |

| | | | |
|---|---|---|---|
| HYFRYDOL | John Scott | 42 | 26 |
| IN CHRIST ALONE (in D and E♭) | Ashley Grote | 43 | 27 |
| IRBY (in F and G) | Benjamin Lamb | 44 | 28 |
| JESUS IS LORD (in G and A♭) | James Whitbourn | 45 | 28, 29 |
| LASST UNS ERFREUEN (in D and E♭) | Christopher Gower | 46 | 29, 30 |
| LAUDA ANIMA | Alan Gray | 69 | 44 |
| LAUDES DOMINI (in C and B♭) | Reginald Thatcher | 47 | 30 |
| LAUDS | John Wilson | 48 | 31 |
| LAUS DEO | Sydney H Nicholson | 49 | 31 |
| LOBE DEN HERREN (in F and G) | Harrison Oxley | 50 | 31, 32 |
| LORD OF THE YEARS | John Barnard | 51 | 32 |
| LUCKINGTON | William Mathias | 52 | 33 |
| LUX EOI | Richard Lloyd | 53 | 33 |
| MACCABAEUS (in E♭ and D) | Malcolm Archer | 54 | 34, 35 |
| MELCOMBE (in E♭ and D) | Alan Gray | 55 | 36 |
| MELITA | Alan Gray | 56 | 36 |
| MENDELSSOHN (in F and G) | David Willcocks | 57 | 37 |
| MERTON (in F and E) | Alan Gray | 58 | 38 |
| MILES LANE | Alan Gray | 59 | 38 |
| MONKLAND | John Wilson | 60 | 39 |
| MONKS GATE | Cyril Winn | 61 | 39 |
| MORNING HYMN | David Willcocks | 62 | 40 |
| MOSCOW | Alan Gray | 63 | 40 |
| NEANDER | Sydney H Nicholson | 64 | 41 |
| NICAEA | James Vivian | 65 | 41 |
| NOEL | David Willcocks | 66 | 42 |
| NUN DANKET (in F and E♭) | William H Harris | 67 | 42, 43 |
| ORIEL | Alan Gray | 68 | 43 |
| PRAISE, MY SOUL | Alan Gray | 69 | 44 |
| PRAXIS PIETATIS (in F and G) | Harrison Oxley | 50 | 31, 32 |
| PUER NOBIS NASCITUR | John Scott | 70 | 44 |
| QUAM DILECTA | John Henderson | 71 | 45 |
| REDHEAD No. 46 | Sydney H Nicholson | 49 | 31 |
| REGENT SQUARE | David Thorne | 72 | 45 |
| REPTON | John Scott | 73 | 46 |
| RICHMOND (in F and G) | Edward Bairstow | 74 | 46, 47 |
| ROCKINGHAM (in D and E♭) | Unknown | 75 | 47 |
| SAFFRON WALDEN | Simon Lole | 76 | 48 |
| ST ALBINUS (in C and B♭) | John Henderson | 77 | 48 |
| ST ANNE | John Scott | 78 | 49 |
| ST CLEMENT (in A♭ and G) | David Blackwell | 79 | 49 |
| ST COLUMBA | Donald Davison | 80 | 50 |
| ST DENIO (in A♭ and G) | Cyril Winn | 81 | 50 |
| ST GEORGE'S WINDSOR | Robert Gower | 82 | 51 |
| ST HELEN | Christopher Gower | 83 | 51 |
| ST MAGNUS | John Wilson | 84 | 52 |
| SEEK YE FIRST | William Llewellyn | 85 | 52 |
| SINE NOMINE | Cyril Winn | 86 | 52 |
| SING HOSANNA (in E♭ and D) | Traditional | 87 | 53 |
| SLANE | John Wilson | 88a | 53 |
| SLANE | David Thorne | 88b | 54 |

| | | | |
|---|---|---|---|
| SONG 34 | Donald Davison | 89 | 54 |
| STUTTGART (in G and F) | Antony Baldwin | 90 | 55 |
| THE SERVANT KING | Ashley Grote | 91 | 55 |
| THORNBURY | David Willcocks | 92 | 56 |
| TRURO (in D and C) | John Wilson | 93 | 56 |
| UNSER HERRSCHER | Sydney H Nicholson | 64 | 41 |
| VENI EMMANUEL (metrical version) | Robert Gower | 94a | 57 |
| VENI EMMANUEL (plainchant version) | Robert Gower | 94b | 57 |
| WAREHAM (in B♭ and A) | Sydney H Nicholson | 95 | 58 |
| WAS LEBET | Donald Davison | 96 | 58 |
| WESTMINSTER ABBEY (in A♭ and G) | John Rutter | 97 | 59 |
| WINCHESTER NEW | Alan Gray | 98 | 60 |
| WINCHESTER OLD | Alan Gray | 99 | 60 |
| WOODLANDS | Richard Lloyd | 100a | 61 |
| WOODLANDS | Benjamin Lamb | 100b | 61 |


## INDEX OF FIRST LINES


| FIRST LINE | NO. | PAGE |
|---|---|---|
| Abide with me; fast falls the eventide | 29 | 20 |
| All creatures of our God and King | 46 | 29, 30 |
| All hail the power of Jesu's name | 59 | 38 |
| All praise to thee, for thou, O King divine | 28 | 19 |
| Alleluia, alleluia, give thanks to the risen Lord | 5 | 5 |
| Alleluia, alleluia! Hearts to heaven and voices raise | 53 | 33 |
| Alleluia, sing to Jesus | 42 | 26 |
| Angel-voices ever singing | 6 | 6 |
| As with gladness men of old | 22 | 16 |
| Awake, awake: fling off the night | 21 | 15 |
| Awake, my soul, and with the sun | 62 | 40 |
| Be thou my guardian and my guide | 3 | 4 |
| Be thou my vision, O Lord of my heart | 88a | 53 |
| Beauty for brokenness | 11 | 9 |
| Blessed city, heavenly Salem | 97 | 59 |
| Bright the vision that delighted | 49 | 31 |
| Christ is alive! Let Christians sing | 93 | 56 |
| Christ is made the sure foundation | 97 | 59 |
| Christ triumphant, ever reigning | 37 | 24 |
| City of God, how broad and far | 74 | 46, 47 |
| Come down, O Love divine | 24 | 17 |
| Come, thou long-expected Jesus (*Cross of Jesus*) | 17 | 12, 13 |
| Come, thou long-expected Jesus (*Stuttgart*) | 90 | 55 |
| Come, thou Redeemer of the earth | 70 | 44 |
| Come, ye faithful, raise the anthem | 64 | 41 |
| Come, ye thankful people, come | 82 | 51 |
| Dear Lord and Father of mankind | 73 | 46 |

| | | |
|---|---|---|
| Earth has many a noble city | 90 | 55 |
| Eternal Father, strong to save | 56 | 36 |
| Faithful one, so unchanging | 30 | 20 |
| Father, Lord of all creation | 1 | 2, 3 |
| Father, we adore you | 32 | 21 |
| Father, we love you, we worship and adore you | 33 | 22 |
| Fight the good fight with all thy might | 25 | 17 |
| For all the saints who from their labours rest | 86 | 52 |
| Forth in the peace of Christ we go | 25 | 17 |
| Forth in thy name, O Lord, I go | 89 | 54 |
| Forty days and forty nights | 9 | 8 |
| From heaven you came, helpless babe | 91 | 55 |
| Give me joy in my heart, keep me praising | 87 | 53 |
| Give me oil in my lamp, keep me burning | 87 | 53 |
| Glorious things of thee are spoken (*Abbot's Leigh*) | 1 | 2, 3 |
| Glorious things of thee are spoken (*Austria*) | 10 | 8 |
| 'Glory to God!' all heaven with joy is ringing | 40 | 25 |
| God is here! As we his people | 12 | 10 |
| God is Love: let heaven adore him | 1 | 2, 3 |
| God rest you merry, gentlemen | 36 | 23 |
| Great is thy faithfulness, O God my Father | 31 | 21 |
| Guide me, O thou great Redeemer (Jehovah) | 19 | 14 |
| Hark, a thrilling voice is sounding | 58 | 38 |
| Hark! the herald-angels sing | 57 | 37 |
| He who would valiant be | 61 | 39 |
| Holy, holy, holy is the Lord | 41 | 26 |
| Holy, holy, holy! Lord God Almighty | 65 | 41 |
| How shall I sing that majesty | 14 | 11 |
| Immortal, invisible, God only wise | 81 | 50 |
| In Christ alone my hope is found | 43 | 27 |
| It came upon the midnight clear | 66 | 42 |
| Jesu, lover of my soul | 2 | 4 |
| Jesus calls us: o'er the tumult | 58 | 38 |
| Jesus Christ is risen today, Alleluia | 26 | 18 |
| Jesus is Lord! Creation's voice proclaims it | 45 | 28, 29 |
| Jesus lives! thy terrors now | 77 | 48 |
| Jesus shall reign where'er the sun | 93 | 56 |
| Jesus, where'er thy people meet | 95 | 58 |
| Just as I am, without one plea | 76 | 48 |
| Let all the world in every corner sing | 52 | 33 |
| Let us, with a gladsome mind | 60 | 39 |
| Lift high the cross, the love of Christ proclaim | 18 | 13 |
| 'Lift up your hearts!' We lift them, Lord, to thee | 100a | 61 |
| Light's abode, celestial Salem | 72 | 45 |
| Lo, he comes with clouds descending | 39 | 25 |
| Lord, enthroned in heavenly splendour | 83 | 51 |
| Lord, for the years your love has kept and guided | 51 | 32 |
| Lord of all hopefulness, Lord of all joy | 88b | 54 |
| Love divine, all loves excelling | 12 | 10 |
| My God, and is thy table spread | 75 | 47 |

| | | |
|---|---|---|
| New every morning is the love | 55 | 36 |
| Now thank we all our God | 67 | 42, 43 |
| O come, all ye faithful | 4 | 5 |
| O come, O come, Emmanuel | 94 | 57 |
| O God, our help in ages past | 78 | 49 |
| O little town of Bethlehem | 34 | 22 |
| O Lord of every shining constellation | 40 | 25 |
| O Love, how deep, how broad, how high | 27 | 18 |
| O perfect Love, all human thought transcending | 40 | 25 |
| O saving Victim, opening wide | 27 | 18 |
| O worship the King, all glorious above | 38 | 24 |
| O worship the Lord in the beauty of holiness | 96 | 58 |
| On Jordan's bank the Baptist's cry | 98 | 60 |
| Once in royal David's city | 44 | 28 |
| Praise, O praise our God and King | 60 | 39 |
| Praise, my soul, the King of heaven | 69 | 44 |
| Praise the Lord! ye heavens, adore him | 10 | 8 |
| Praise to the Holiest in the height | 35 | 23 |
| Praise to the Lord, the Almighty, the King of creation | 50 | 31, 32 |
| Rejoice, O land, in God thy might | 95 | 58 |
| Ride on, ride on in majesty | 98 | 60 |
| Seek ye first the kingdom of God | 85 | 52 |
| Sing we of the blessed Mother | 1 | 2, 3 |
| Soul of my Saviour, sanctify my breast | 7 | 6, 7 |
| Stand up, and bless the Lord | 13 | 11 |
| Tell out, my soul, the greatness of the Lord | 100b | 61 |
| The Church's one foundation | 8 | 7 |
| The day thou gavest, Lord, is ended | 79 | 49 |
| The head that once was crowned with thorns | 84 | 52 |
| The heavenly Word proceeding forth | 27 | 18 |
| The King of love my shepherd is (*Dominus regit me*) | 23 | 16, 17 |
| The King of love my shepherd is (*St Columba*) | 80 | 50 |
| The kingdom of God is justice and joy | 38 | 24 |
| The Lord's my shepherd, I'll not want | 16 | 12 |
| There's a spirit in the air | 48 | 31 |
| There's a wideness in God's mercy | 15 | 12 |
| Thine be the glory, risen, conquering Son | 54 | 34, 35 |
| Thou whose almighty word | 63 | 40 |
| Thy hand, O God, has guided | 92 | 56 |
| 'Tis good, Lord, to be here | 13 | 11 |
| To the name of our salvation | 68 | 43 |
| We love the place, O God | 71 | 45 |
| When I survey the wondrous cross | 75 | 47 |
| When, in our music, God is glorified | 28 | 19 |
| When morning gilds the skies | 47 | 30 |
| While shepherds watched their flocks by night | 99 | 60 |
| Who would true valour see | 61 | 39 |
| Ye holy angels bright | 20 | 14, 15 |
| Ye that know the Lord is gracious | 42 | 26 |
| Ye watchers and ye holy ones | 46 | 29, 30 |

# The Oxford Book of Descants

# 1a ABBOT'S LEIGH (in C)

Glorious things of thee are spoken
*Father, Lord of all creation*
God is Love: let heaven adore him
*Sing we of the blessed Mother*

Descant by Antony Baldwin

Sa - viour, if of Zi - on's ci - ty I through grace a
*Ho - ly Spi - rit, rush - ing, burn - ing wind and flame of*
God is Love: and though with blind - ness sin af - flicts the
*Sing the chief - est joy of Ma - ry when on earth her*

mem - ber am, let the world de - ride or pi - ty,
*Pen - te - cost, fire our hearts a - fresh with yearn-ing*
souls of men, God's e - ter - nal lov - ing - kind-ness
*work was done, and the Lord of all cre - a - tion*

I will glo - ry in thy name; fa - ding is the
*to re - gain what we have lost. May your love u -*
holds and guides them e - ven then. Sin and death and
*brought her to his heaven - ly home: vir - gin mo - ther,*

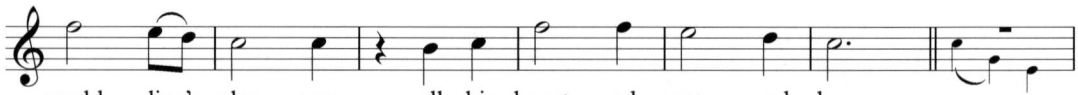

world - ling's plea - sure, all his boast - ed pomp and show;
*-nite our ac - tion, ne - ver - more to speak a - lone:*
hell shall ne - ver o'er us fi - nal tri - umph gain;
*Ma - ry bless - ed, raised on high and crowned with grace,*

so - lid joys and trea - sure none but Zi - on's child - ren know.
*God, a - bo - lish fac - tion, God, through us your love make known.*
God is Love, for ev - er o'er the u - ni - verse must reign.
*may your Son, re - deem - er, grant us all to see his face.*

*Abbot's Leigh* by Cyril Vincent Taylor (1907–91) © 1942 Oxford University Press
Descant by Antony Baldwin (b. 1957) © 2006 Oxford University Press
First text: 'Glorious things of thee are spoken' by John Newton (1725–1807)
Second text: 'Father, Lord of all creation' by Stewart Cross (1928–89) © Mrs Mary Cross
Third text: 'God is Love: let heaven adore him' by Timothy Rees (1874–1939)
Fourth text: 'Sing we of the blessed Mother' by George B Timms (1910–97) © Oxford University Press

# 1b ABBOT'S LEIGH (in D)

Glorious things of thee are spoken
*Father, Lord of all creation*
God is Love: let heaven adore him
*Sing we of the blessed Mother*

Descant by Antony Baldwin

Sa - viour, if of Zi - on's ci - ty I through grace a
*Ho - ly Spi - rit, rush - ing, burn - ing wind and flame of*
God is Love: and though with blind - ness sin af - flicts the
*Sing the chief - est joy of Ma - ry when on earth her*

mem - ber am, let the world de - ride or pi - ty,
*Pen - te - cost, fire our hearts a - fresh with yearn - ing*
souls of men, God's e - ter - nal lov - ing - kind - ness
*work was done, and the Lord of all cre - a - tion*

I will glo - ry in thy name; fa - ding is the
*to re - gain what we have lost. May your love u -*
holds and guides them e - ven then. Sin and death and
*brought her to his heaven - ly home: vir - gin mo - ther,*

world - ling's plea - sure, all his boast - ed pomp and show;
*-nite our ac - tion, ne - ver - more to speak a - lone:*
hell shall ne - ver o'er us fi - nal tri - umph gain;
*Ma - ry bless - ed, raised on high and crowned with grace,*

so - lid joys and trea - sure none but Zi - on's child - ren know.
*God, a - bo - lish fac - tion, God, through us your love make known.*
God is Love, for ev - er o'er the u - ni - verse must reign.
*may your Son, re - deem - er, grant us all to see his face.*

*Abbot's Leigh* by Cyril Vincent Taylor (1907–91) © 1942 Oxford University Press
Descant by Antony Baldwin (b. 1957) © 2006 Oxford University Press
First text: 'Glorious things of thee are spoken' by John Newton (1725–1807)
Second text: 'Father, Lord of all creation' by Stewart Cross (1928–89) © Mrs Mary Cross
Third text: 'God is Love: let heaven adore him' by Timothy Rees (1874–1939)
Fourth text: 'Sing we of the blessed Mother' by George B Timms (1910–97) © Oxford University Press

# 2 ABERYSTWYTH

Jesu, lover of my soul

Descant by Alan Gray

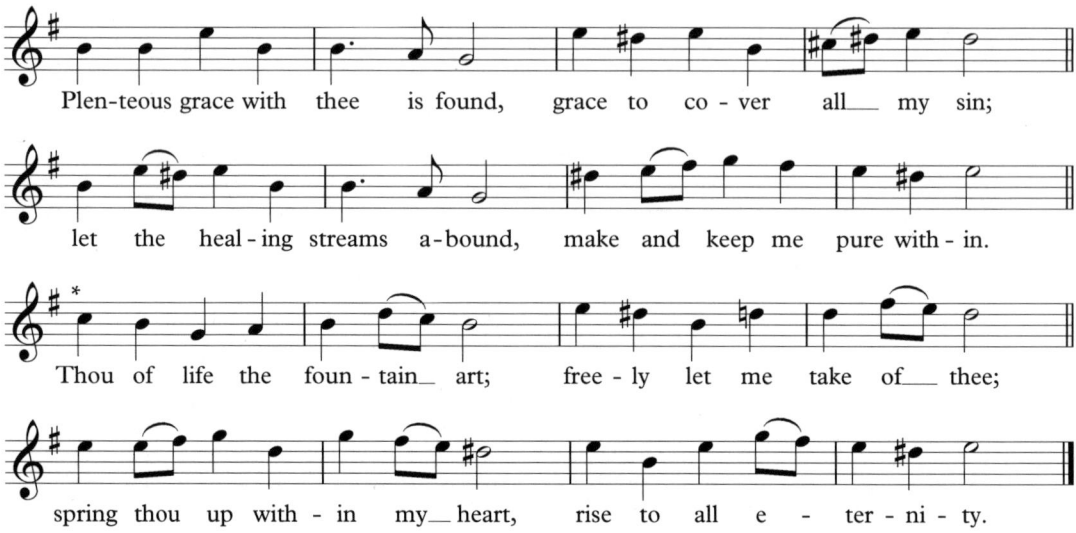


* As an alternative (and at Alan Gray's suggestion), start the descant at this point.
*Aberystwyth* by Joseph Parry (1841–1903)
Descant by Alan Gray (1855–1935)
Text: 'Jesu, lover of my soul' by Charles Wesley (1707–88)

# 3a & b ABRIDGE (in D and C)

Be thou my guardian and my guide

Descant by Christopher Gower

3a in D

3b in C

*Abridge* by Isaac Smith (1734–1805)
Descant by Christopher Gower (b. 1939) © 1990 Kevin Mayhew Ltd. Reproduced by permission; Licence Nr 217011/1
<www.kevinmayhew.com>
Text: 'Be thou my guardian and my guide' by Isaac Williams (1802–65)

# 4 ADESTE, FIDELES

O come, all ye faithful

Descant by David Willcocks

*Adeste fideles* possibly by John Francis Wade (*c.*1711–86)
Descant by David Willcocks (b. 1919) © 1961 Oxford University Press
Text: 'O come, all ye faithful' translated by Frederick Oakeley (1802–80) from 18th-century Latin

# 5 ALLELUIA No. 1

Alleluia, alleluia, give thanks to the risen Lord

Descant by Anthony F Carver
and Donald Davison

Melody and words by Donald E Fishel (b. 1950)
Descant by Anthony F Carver (b. 1947) and Donald Davison (b. 1937)
© 1973 International Liturgy Publications (ILP) PO Box 50476, Nashville, Tennessee 37205 USA. Administered by Song Solutions CopyCare <www.songsolutions.org>

# 6a & b ANGEL VOICES (in D and C)

Angel-voices ever singing

Descant by John Cooke

6a in D

6b in C

*Angel Voices* by E G Monk (1819–1900)
Descant by John Cooke (1930–95) © The Estate of John Cooke
Text: 'Angel-voices ever singing' by Francis Pott (1832–1909)

# 7a ANIMA CHRISTI (in F)

Soul of my Saviour, sanctify my breast

Descant by David Willcocks

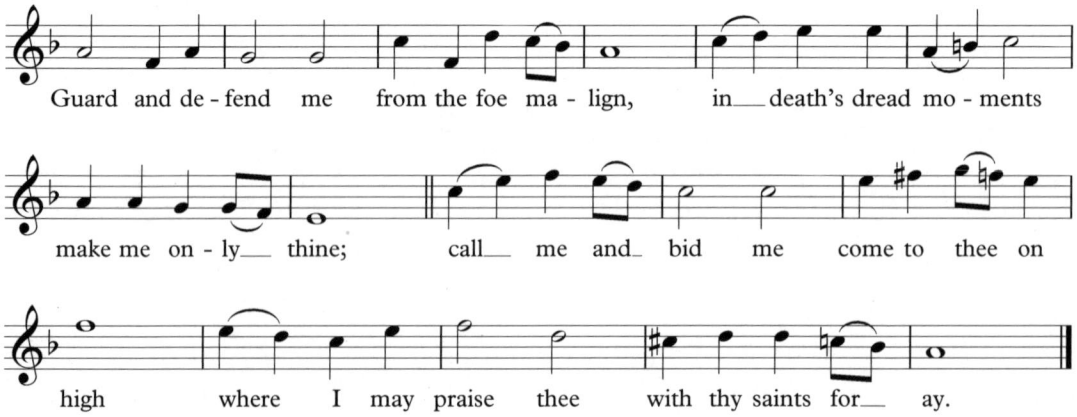


*Anima Christi* by William Maher (1823–77)
Descant by David Willcocks (b. 1919) © 2012 Oxford University Press
Text: 'Soul of my Saviour, sanctify my breast'—anonymous translation of 14th-century Latin

# 7b ANIMA CHRISTI (in G)

Soul of my Saviour, sanctify my breast

Descant by David Willcocks

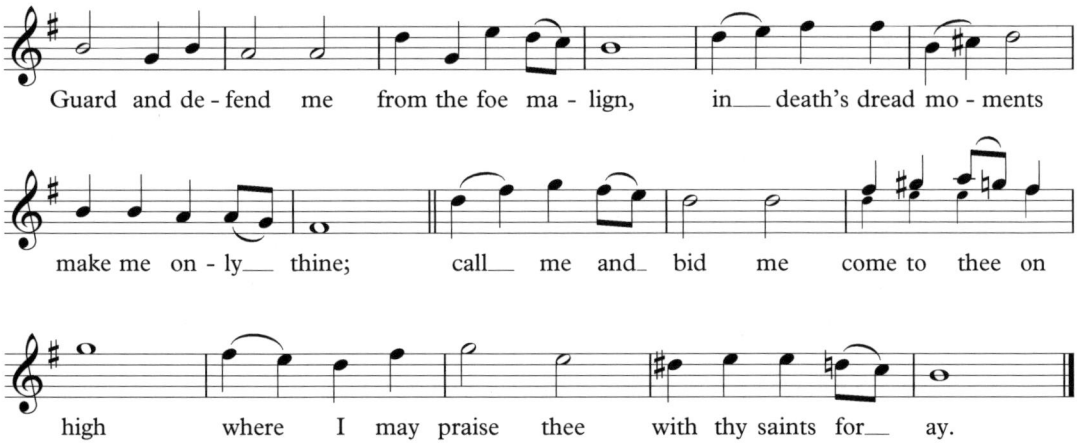


*Anima Christi* by William Maher (1823–77)
Descant by David Willcocks (b. 1919) © 2012 Oxford University Press
Text: 'Soul of my Saviour, sanctify my breast'—anonymous translation of 14th-century Latin

# 8 AURELIA

The Church's one foundation

Descant by Adrian Lucas

*Aurelia* by S S Wesley (1810–76)
Descant by Adrian Lucas (b. 1962) © 2012 Oxford University Press
Text: 'The Church's one foundation' by Samuel J Stone (1839–1900)

# 9 AUS DER TIEFE (HEINLEIN)

Forty days and forty nights

Descant by James Vivian

*Aus der Tiefe* or *Heinlein* possibly by Martin Herbst (1654–81)
Descant by James Vivian (b. 1974) © 2012 Oxford University Press
Text: 'Forty days and forty nights' by George H Smyttan (1822–70) and Francis Pott (1832–1909)

# 10a & b AUSTRIA (in E♭ and F)

Praise the Lord! ye heavens, adore him
*Glorious things of thee are spoken*

Descant by Thomas H Ingham

10a in E♭

10b in F

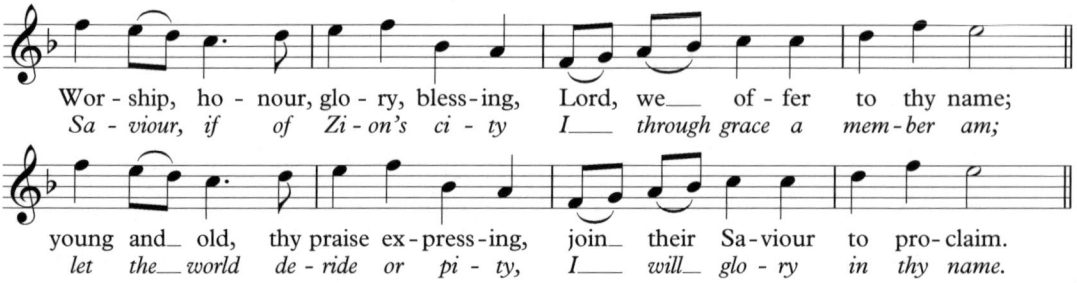


*Austria* by Franz Joseph Haydn (1732–1809)
Descant by Thomas H Ingham (1878–1948) © 1925 Oxford University Press
First text: 'Praise the Lord! ye heavens, adore him'—third verse by Edward Osler (1798–1863)
Second text: 'Glorious things of thee are spoken' by John Newton (1725–1807)

# 11 BEAUTY FOR BROKENNESS (GOD OF THE POOR)

Beauty for brokenness

Descant by Ashley Grote

Melody and words by Graham Kendrick (b. 1950)
Descant by Ashley Grote (b. 1982)
© 1993 Graham Kendrick / Make Way Music Ltd, PO Box 320, Tunbridge Wells, TN2 9DE, UK. <www.grahamkendrick.co.uk>
Used by permission

# 12a & b BLAENWERN (in G and F)

Love divine, all loves excelling
*God is here! As we his people*

Descant by John Scott

12a in G

12b in F



*Blaenwern* by William P Rowlands (1860–1937)
Descant by John Scott (b. 1956) © 2001 Banks Music Publications. Reproduced by permission
First text: 'Love divine, all loves excelling' by Charles Wesley (1707–88)
Second text: 'God is here! As we his people' by F Pratt Green (1903–2000)

# 13a & b CARLISLE (in E♭ and D)

Stand up, and bless the Lord

*'Tis good, Lord, to be here*

Descant by Sydney H Nicholson

13a in E♭

*Carlisle* by Charles Lockhart (1745–1815)
Descant by Sydney H Nicholson (1875–1947) © The Royal School of Church Music. Used by permission
First text: 'Stand up, and bless the Lord' by James Montgomery (1771–1854)
Second text: ''Tis good, Lord, to be here' by J Armitage Robinson (1858–1933)

# 14 COE FEN

How shall I sing that majesty

Descant by Kenneth Naylor

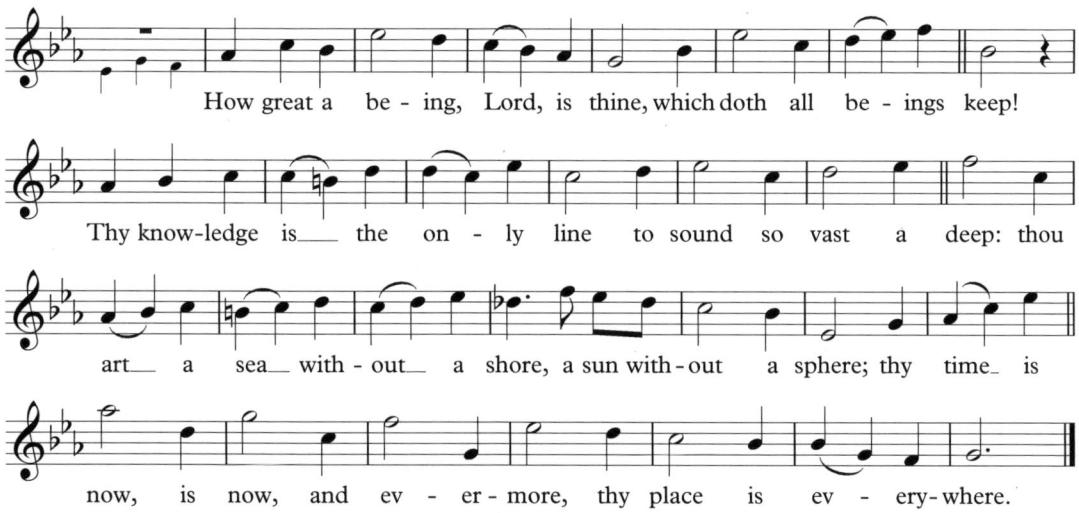


Hymn tune and descant by Kenneth Naylor (1931–91) © The Estate of Kenneth Nicholson Naylor. Administered by Oxford University Press
Text: 'How shall I sing that majesty' by John Mason (*c*.1645–94)

# 15 CORVEDALE

There's a wideness in God's mercy

Descant by Maurice Bevan

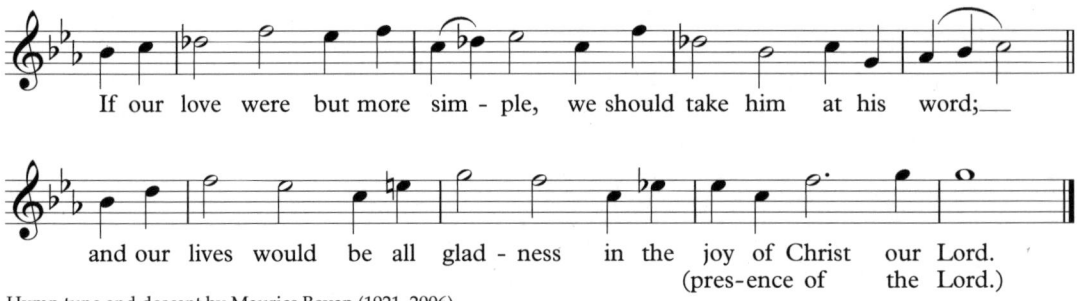


Hymn tune and descant by Maurice Bevan (1921–2006)
© 1993 Cathedral Music Ltd, King Charles Cottage, Racton, Chichester, West Sussex PO18 9DT
Text: 'There's a wideness in God's mercy' by Frederick W Faber (1814–63)

# 16 CRIMOND

The Lord's my shepherd, I'll not want

Descant by Donald Davison

*Crimond* probably by David Grant (1833–93)
Descant by Donald Davison (b. 1937) © 2000 Oxford University Place
Text: 'The Lord's my shepherd, I'll not want' from the *Scottish Psalter* 1650

# 17a CROSS OF JESUS (in G)

Come, thou long-expected Jesus

Descant by Paul Leddington Wright

*Cross of Jesus* by John Stainer (1840–1901)
Descant by Paul Leddington Wright (b. 1951) © 2012 Oxford University Press
Text: 'Come, thou long-expected Jesus' by Charles Wesley (1707–88)

# 17b CROSS OF JESUS (in F)

Come, thou long-expected Jesus

Descant by Paul Leddington Wright

*Cross of Jesus* by John Stainer (1840–1901)
Descant by Paul Leddington Wright (b. 1951) © 2012 Oxford University Press
Text: 'Come, thou long-expected Jesus' by Charles Wesley (1707–88)

# 18a & b CRUCIFER (in D and C)

Lift high the cross, the love of Christ proclaim

Descant by Harold Darke

18a in D

18b in C

*Crucifer* by Sydney H Nicholson (1875–1947) © Hymns Ancient & Modern Ltd. Used by permission
Descant by Harold Darke (1888–1976) © The Estate of Harold Darke. Used by permission
Text: 'Lift high the cross' by G W Kitchin (1827–1912) and M R Newbolt (1874–1956)

# 19 CWM RHONDDA

Guide me, O thou great Redeemer (Jehovah)

Descant by John Scott

*Cwm Rhondda* by John Hughes (1873–1932)
Descant by John Scott (b. 1956) © 2012 Oxford University Press
Text: 'Guide me, O thou great Redeemer' translated from the Welsh of William Williams (1717–91)

# 20a DARWALL'S 148th (in D)

Ye holy angels bright

Descant from *Hymns Ancient & Modern Revised*
by Sydney H Nicholson

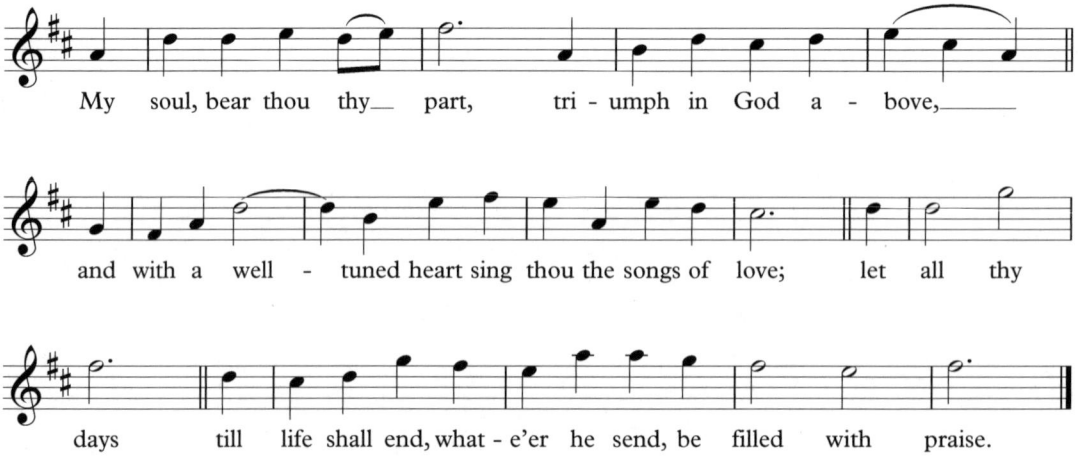


*Darwall's 148th* by John Darwall (1731–89)
Descant from *Hymns Ancient & Modern Revised* by Sydney H Nicholson (1875–1947) © Hymns Ancient & Modern Ltd. Used by permission
Text: 'Ye holy angels bright' by Richard Baxter (1615–91)

## 20b DARWALL'S 148th (in C)

Ye holy angels bright

Descant from *Hymns Ancient & Modern Revised*
by Sydney H Nicholson

My soul, bear thou thy part, tri - umph in God a - bove,

and with a well - tuned heart sing thou the songs of love; let all thy

days till life shall end, what - e'er he send, be filled with praise.

*Darwall's 148th* by John Darwall (1731–89)
Descant from *Hymns Ancient & Modern Revised* by Sydney H Nicholson (1875–1947) © Hymns Ancient & Modern Ltd. Used by permission
Text: 'Ye holy angels bright' by Richard Baxter (1615–91)

## 21a & b DEUS TUORUM MILITUM (in C and B♭)

Awake, awake: fling off the night

Descant by Simon Lole

21a in C

Then sing for joy each day; thanks for ev - 'ry-thing al - way.

Lift your hearts; with one ac-cord praise God through Je - sus Christ our Lord.

21b in B♭

Then sing for joy each day; thanks for ev - 'ry-thing al - way.

Lift your hearts; with one ac-cord praise God through Je - sus Christ our Lord.

*Deus tuorum militum* from *Grenoble Antiphoner* 1753
Descant by Simon Lole (b. 1957) © 2012 Oxford University Press
Text: 'Awake, awake: fling off the night' by J R Peacey (1896–1971) © The Revd Mary J Hancock

# 22a & b DIX (in A♭ and G)

As with gladness men of old

Descant by John Wilson

22a in A♭

22b in G

*Dix* adapted from a chorale by Conrad Kocher (1786–1872)
Descant by John Wilson (1905–92) © The Estate of John Wilson. Administered by Oxford University Press
Text: 'As with gladness men of old' by William Chatterton Dix (1837–98)

# 23a DOMINUS REGIT ME (in G)

The King of love my shepherd is

Descant from *Hymns Ancient & Modern*
probably by Sydney H Nicholson

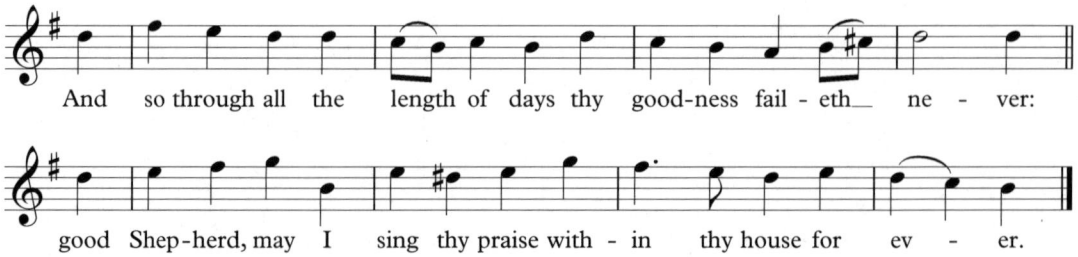


*Dominus regit me* by John Bacchus Dykes (1823–76). Descant from *Hymns Ancient & Modern Revised* probably by Sydney H Nicholson (1875–1947). © Hymns Ancient & Modern Ltd. Used by permission
Text: 'The King of love my shepherd is' by Henry Williams Baker (1821–77)

# 23b DOMINUS REGIT ME (in F)

The King of love my shepherd is

Descant from *Hymns Ancient & Modern*
probably by Sydney H Nicholson

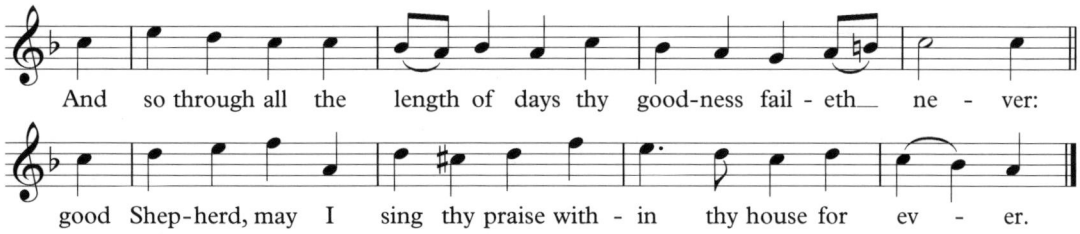


*Dominus regit me* by John Bacchus Dykes (1823–76). Descant from *Hymns Ancient & Modern Revised* probably by Sydney H Nicholson (1875–1947). © Hymns Ancient & Modern Ltd. Used by permission
Text: 'The King of love my shepherd is' by Henry Williams Baker (1821–77)

# 24 DOWN AMPNEY

Come down, O Love divine

Descant by David Willcocks

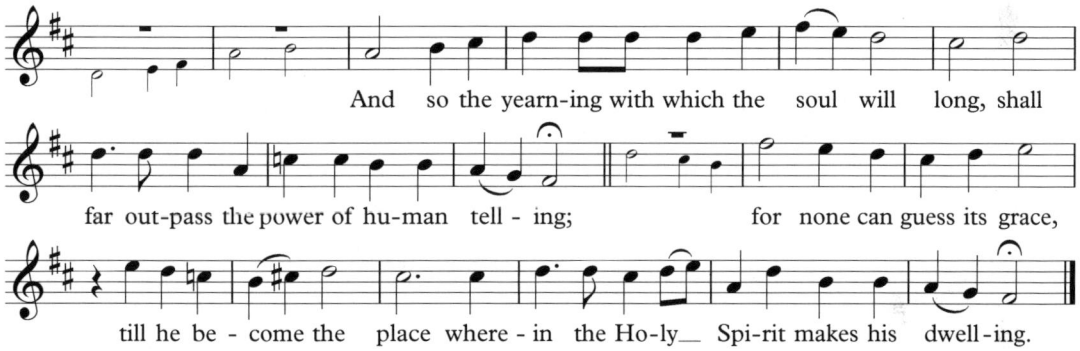


*Down Ampney* by Ralph Vaughan Williams (1872–1958) from *The English Hymnal*. Reproduced by permission of Oxford University Press. All rights reserved. Descant by David Willcocks (b. 1919) © 2012 Oxford University Press
Text: 'Come down, O Love divine' translated from the Italian of Bianco da Siena (d. 1434)

# 25 DUKE STREET

Fight the good fight with all thy might
*Forth in the peace of Christ we go*

Descant by Philip Moore

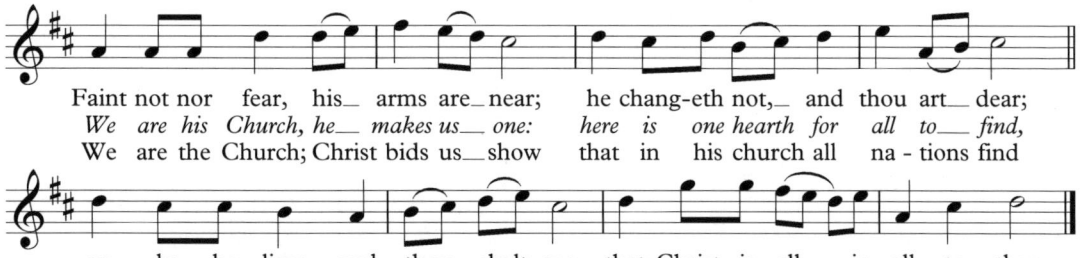


*Duke Street* attributed to John Hatton (d. 1793). Descant by Philip Moore (b. 1943)
© 1996 Kevin Mayhew Ltd. Reproduced by permission; Licence Nr 217011/1 <www.kevinmayhew.com>
First text: 'Fight the good fight with all thy might' by John S B Monsell (1811–75). Second and third texts: 'Forth in the peace of Christ we go' by James Quinn (1919–2010) © 1969 & 1987 Continuum International Publishing Group

# 26 EASTER HYMN

Jesus Christ is risen today, Alleluia

Descant by John Rutter

*Easter Hymn* adapted from *Lyra Davidica* 1708
Descant by John Rutter (b. 1945) © 2000 Collegium Music Publications
Text: 'Jesus Christ is risen today, Alleluia' from *Lyra Davidica* 1708

# 27 EISENACH

O Love, how deep, how broad, how high
*The heavenly Word proceeding forth* (*O saving Victim, opening wide*)

Descant by Harrison Oxley

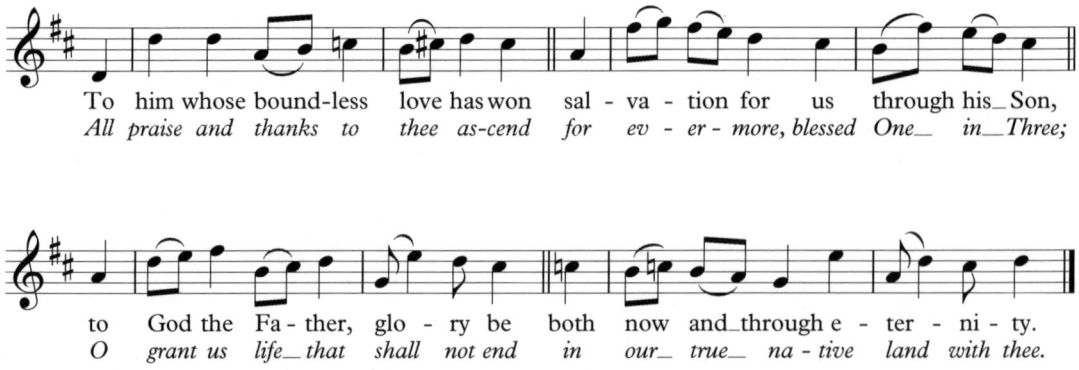


*Eisenach* by Johann Schein (1586–1630)
Descant by Harrison Oxley (1933–2009) © 1996 Kevin Mayhew Ltd. Reproduced by permission; Licence Nr 217011/1
<www.kevinmayhew.com>
First text: 'O Love, how deep, how broad, how high' tr. by Benjamin Webb (1819–85) from 15th-century Latin
Second text: 'The heavenly Word, proceeding forth' tr. by John Mason Neale (1818–66) from Thomas Aquinas

# 28a & b ENGLEBERG (in F and G)

When, in our music, God is glorified

*All praise to thee, for thou, O King divine*

Descant by David Willcocks

28a in F

Let ev - ery in - stru-ment be tuned for praise! Let all re -
*Let ev - ery tongue con - fess with one ac - cord in heaven and*

-joice who have a voice to raise! And may God give us
*earth that Je - sus Christ is Lord; and God the Fa - ther*

*cresc.*

faith to sing al - ways: Al - le - lu - ia!
*be by all a - dored: Al - le - lu - ia!*

28b in G

Let ev - ery in - stru-ment be tuned for praise! Let all re -
*Let ev - ery tongue con - fess with one ac - cord in heaven and*

-joice who have a voice to raise! And may God give us
*earth that Je - sus Christ is Lord; and God the Fa - ther*

*cresc.*

faith to sing al - ways: Al - le - lu - ia!
*be by all a - dored: Al - le - lu - ia!*

*Engleberg* by Charles Villiers Stanford (1852–1924)
Descant by David Willcocks (b. 1919) © 2012 Oxford University Press
First text: 'When, in our music, God is glorified' by F Pratt Green (1903–2000)
Second text: 'All praise to thee, for thou, O King divine' by F Bland Tucker (1895–1984)

# 29 EVENTIDE

Abide with me; fast falls the eventide

Adapted from a choir arrangement
by David Willcocks

*Eventide* by William Henry Monk (1823–89)
Descant by David Willcocks (b. 1919) © 1976 Oxford University Press
Text: 'Abide with me; fast falls the eventide' by Henry Francis Lyte (1793–1847)

# 30 FAITHFUL ONE

Faithful one, so unchanging

Descant by David Thorne

Melody and words by Brian Doerksen (b. 1965)
Descant by David Thorne (b. 1950)
© 1989 Vineyard Songs & ION Publishing. Administered by Song Solutions CopyCare <www.songsolutions.org>

## 31a & b FAITHFULNESS (in E♭ and D)

Great is thy faithfulness, O God my Father

Descant by Paul Leddington Wright and Robert Prizeman

31a in E♭

31b in D

*Faithfulness* (or *Great is thy faithfulness*) by William M Runyan (1870–1957). Descant by Paul Leddington Wright (b. 1951) and Robert Prizeman (b. 1952). Text: 'Great is thy faithfulness, O God my Father' by Thomas Chisholm (1866–1960).
Music and words copyright © 1923 renewed 1951 and this descant © 2012 Hope Publishing Co., Carol Stream, IL 60188 USA. All rights reserved. Used by permission

## 32 FATHER, WE ADORE YOU

Father, we adore you

Descant by William Llewellyn

Melody and words by Terrye Coelho (b. 1952)
Descant by William Llewellyn (b. 1925)
© 1972 Maranatha! Music / CCCM Music / Music Services. Administered by Song Solutions CopyCare <www.songsolutions.org>

# 33 FATHER, WE LOVE YOU

Father, we love you, we worship and adore you

Descant by William Llewellyn

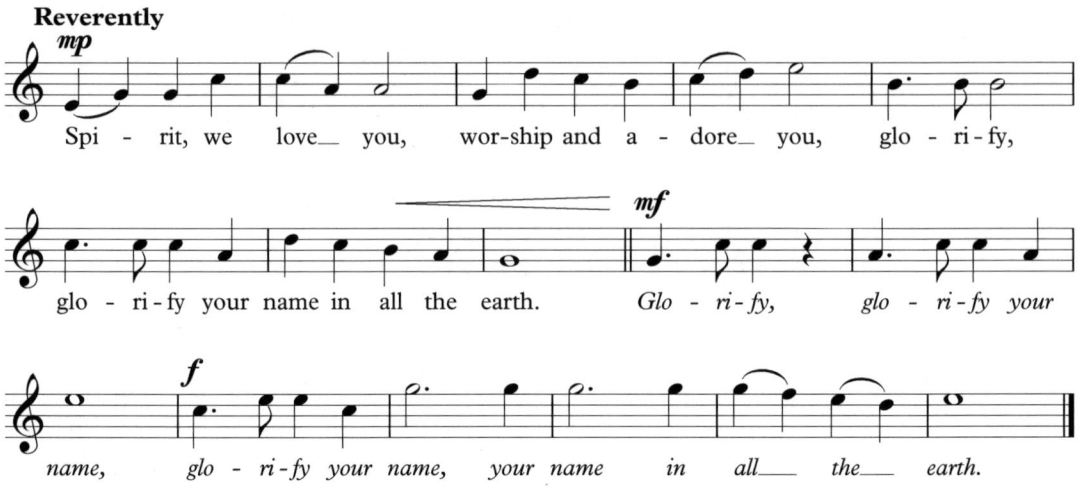


Melody and words by Donna Adkins (b. 1940)
Descant by William Llewellyn (b. 1925)
© 1976/1981 CCCM Music & Maranatha! Music / Universal Music (Print/Sync rights in the UK/Eire only by Small Stone Media BV, Holland). Administered by Song Solutions Daybreak <www.songsolutions.org>

# 34 FOREST GREEN

O little town of Bethlehem

Descant by Thomas Armstrong

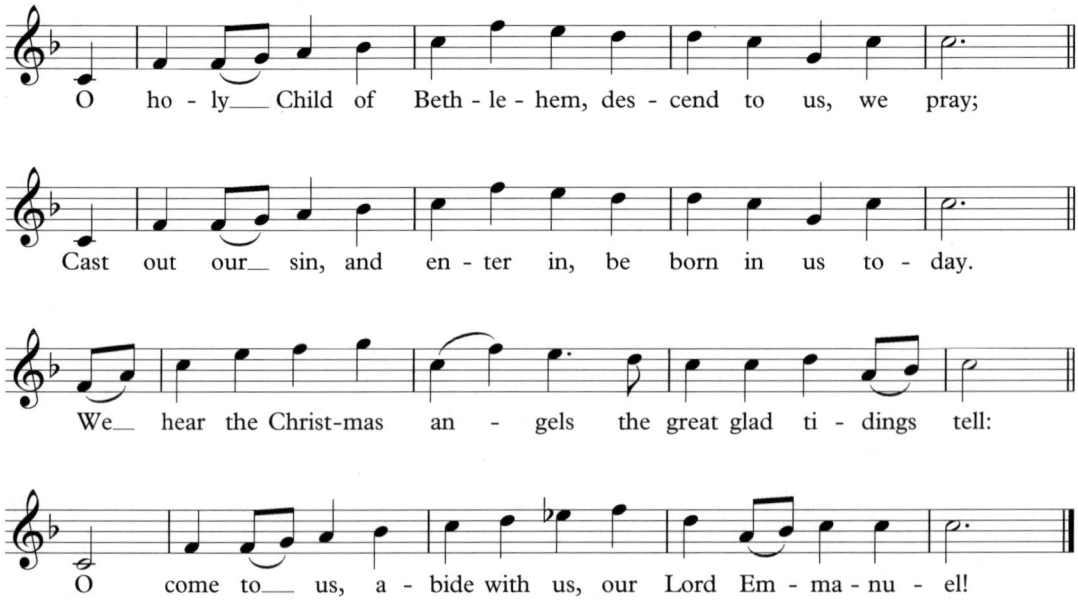


*Forest Green*—English traditional melody collected, adapted, and arranged by Ralph Vaughan Williams (1872–1958) from *The English Hymnal*. Reproduced by permission of Oxford University Press. All rights reserved
Descant by Thomas Armstrong (1898–1994) © The Royal School of Church Music. Used by permission
Text: 'O little town of Bethlehem' by Phillips Brooks (1835–93)

# 35a & b GERONTIUS (in A♭ and G)

Praise to the Holiest in the height

Descant by Robert Gower

35a in A♭

35b in G

*Gerontius* by John Bacchus Dykes (1823–76)
Descant by Robert Gower (b. 1952) © 2012 Oxford University Press
Text: 'Praise to the Holiest in the height' by John Henry Newman (1801–90)

# 36 GOD REST YOU MERRY

God rest you merry, gentlemen

Descant by Christopher Robinson

Descant by Christopher Robinson (b. 1936) © 2012 Oxford University Press
Tune and words—English traditional carol

# 37 GUITING POWER

Christ triumphant, ever reigning

Descant by John Barnard

Our hearts and voi - ces rais - ing through the a - ges long,

up-on you gaz - ing, this shall be our song: *Yours the*

*glo - ry and the crown, the high re - nown, the e - ter - nal name!*

Hymn tune and descant by John Barnard (b. 1948) © John Barnard/Jubilate Hymns
Text: 'Christ triumphant, ever reigning' by Michael Saward (b. 1932) © Michael Saward/Jubilate Hymns
Administered by the Jubilate Group, 4 Thorpe Park Road, Torquay TQ2 6RX. <copyrightmanager@jubilate.co.uk>
Used by permission

# 38 HANOVER

O worship the King, all glorious above

*The kingdom of God is justice and joy*

Descant by Alan Gray

O mea - sure - less might, in - eff - a - ble love, while
*God's king - dom is come, the gift and the goal, in*

an - gels de - light to hymn thee a - bove,
*Je - sus be - gun, in hea - ven made whole;*

thy hum - bler cre - a - tion, though fee - ble their lays, with
*the heirs of the king - dom shall ans - wer his call, and*

true a - do - ra - tion shall sing to thy praise.
*all things cry 'Glo - ry!' to God all in all.*

*Hanover* probably by William Croft (1678–1727)
Descant by Alan Gray (1855–1935)
First text: 'O worship the King, all glorious above' by Robert Grant (1780–1838)
Second text: 'The kingdom of God is justice and joy' by Bryn Rees (1911–83) © Alexander Scott

# 39 HELMSLEY

Lo, he comes with clouds descending

Descant by John Rutter

*Helmsley* included in John Wesley's *Select Hymns* 1765. Descant by John Rutter (b. 1945) © 2000 Collegium Music Publications
Text: 'Lo, he comes with clouds descending' by John Cennick (1718–55) and Charles Wesley (1707–88)

# 40 HIGHWOOD

'Glory to God!' all heaven with joy is ringing
*O Lord of every shining constellation*
O perfect Love, all human thought transcending

Descant by Robert Gower

*Highwood* by Richard R Terry (1865–1938). Descant by Robert Gower (b. 1952) © 2012 Oxford University Press
First text: '"Glory to God!" all heaven with joy is ringing' by John E Bowers (b. 1923) © John E Bowers
Second text: 'O Lord of every shining constellation' by Albert F Bayly (1901–84) © Oxford University Press
Third text: 'O perfect Love, all human thought transcending' by Dorothy F Gurney (1858–1932)

# 41a & b HOLY IS THE LORD (in A and G)

Holy, holy, holy is the Lord

Descant by Ashley Grote

41a in A

Ho - ly, ho - ly, ho - ly is the Lord: God, the
*Glo - ry, glo - ry, glo - ry to the Lord: God, the*

1. 2.

Lord God al - might - y! - might - y! who was, and is, and is
*Lord God al - might - y! - might - y! who was, and is, and is*

to come: ho - ly, ho - ly, ho - ly is the Lord!
*to come: glo - ry, glo - ry, glo - ry to the Lord!*

41b in G

Ho - ly, ho - ly, ho - ly is the Lord: God, the
*Glo - ry, glo - ry, glo - ry to the Lord: God, the*

1. 2.

Lord God al - might - y! - might - y! who was, and is, and is
*Lord God al - might - y! - might - y! who was, and is, and is*

to come: ho - ly, ho - ly, ho - ly is the Lord!
*to come: glo - ry, glo - ry, glo - ry to the Lord!*

Music and words anon. (words based on Revelation 4: 8 & 11). Descant by Ashley Grote (b. 1982) © 2012 Oxford University Press

# 42 HYFRYDOL

Alleluia, sing to Jesus

*Ye that know the Lord is gracious*

Descant by John Scott

Al - le - lu - ia, King e - ter - nal, thee the Lord of
*Tell the praise of him who called you out of dark - ness*

lords we own; al - le - lu - ia, born of Ma - ry, earth thy
*in - to light, broke the fet - ters that en - thralled you, gave you*

*Hyfrydol* by Rowland Hugh Prichard (1811–87). Descant by John Scott (b. 1956) © 2001 Banks Music Publications. Reproduced by permission. First text: 'Alleluia, sing to Jesus' by William Chatterton Dix (1837–98). Second text: 'Ye that know the Lord is gracious' by Cyril A Alington (1872–1955) © Hymns Ancient & Modern Ltd

## 43a & b IN CHRIST ALONE (in D and E♭)

In Christ alone my hope is found

Descant by Ashley Grote

43a in D

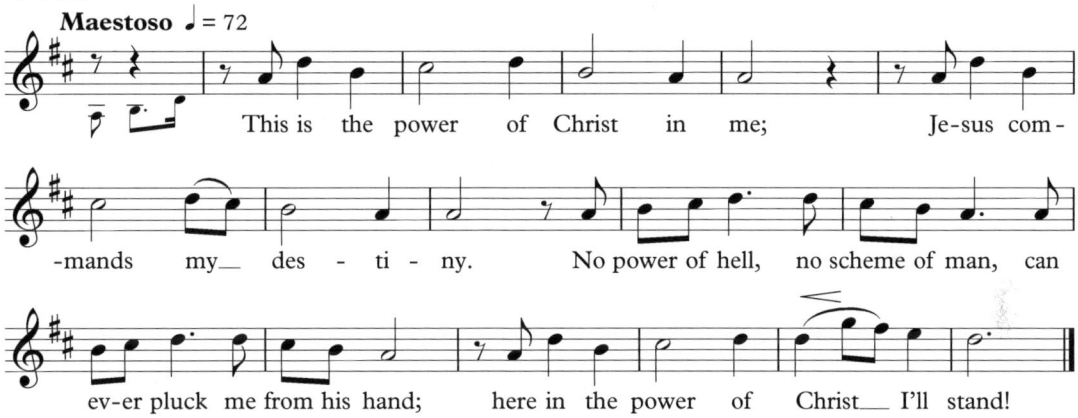


43b in E♭

Melody and words by Stuart Townend (b. 1963) and Keith Getty (b. 1974). Descant by Ashley Grote (b. 1982)
© 2001 Thankyou Music / Administered by worshiptogether.com Songs, excluding UK & Europe, administered by kingswaysongs, a division of David C Cook <tym@kingsway.co.uk> Used by permission

# 44a & b IRBY (in F and G)

Once in royal David's city

Descant by Benjamin Lamb

44a in F

Not in that poor low - ly sta - ble, ox - en stand-ing by;

we shall see him in hea - ven, set at God's right hand on high.

Where like stars his child-ren crowned all in white shall wait a - round.

44b in G

Not in that poor low - ly sta - ble, ox - en stand-ing by;

we shall see him in hea - ven, set at God's right hand on high.

Where like stars his child-ren crowned all in white shall wait a - round.

*Irby* by Henry Gauntlett (1805–76)
Descant by Benjamin Lamb (b. 1974) © 2012 Oxford University Press
Text: 'Once in royal David's city' by Cecil Frances Alexander (1818–95)

# 45a JESUS IS LORD (in G)

Jesus is Lord! Creation's voice proclaims it

Descant by James Whitbourn

*Ah ah

ah ah

*Je-sus is Lord, Je-sus is Lord! Praise him, praise him for Je-sus is Lord!*

* 'Ah' should be pronounced as in 'u' in under.

Melody and words by David Mansell (b. 1936). Descant by James Whitbourn (b. 1963). © 1982 Authentic Publishing administered by kingswaysongs, a division of David C Cook <tym@kingsway.co.uk> Used by permission

# 45b JESUS IS LORD (in A♭)

Jesus is Lord! Creation's voice proclaims it

Descant by James Whitbourn

*Ah ah

ah ah

*Je-sus is Lord, Je-sus is Lord! Praise him, praise him for Je-sus is Lord!*

* 'Ah' should be pronounced as in 'u' in under.

Melody and words by David Mansell (b. 1936). Descant by James Whitbourn (b. 1963). © 1982 Authentic Publishing administered by kingswaysongs, a division of David C Cook <tym@kingsway.co.uk> Used by permission

# 46a LASST UNS ERFREUEN (in D)

All creatures of our God and King

*Ye watchers and ye holy ones*

Descant by Christopher Gower

Let all things their cre-a-tor bless, and wor-ship him. O

*O friends, in glad-ness let us sing, su - per-nal an-thems, al -*

praise him, al-le-lu-ia! Praise the Fa-ther,

*- le - lu - ia, al - le - lu - ia! God the Fa - ther,*

praise the Son, Spi-rit, Three in One: O praise him, O

*God the Son, Spi-rit, Three in One: Al - le - lu - ia, al-le-*

praise him, Al-le-lu-ia, al-le-lu-ia, al-le-lu - - ia!

*-lu - ia, al-le-lu - ia, al-le-lu-ia, al-le-lu - - ia!*

*Lasst uns erfreuen* arr. by Ralph Vaughan Williams (1872–1958) from *The English Hymnal*. Reproduced by permission of Oxford University Press. All rights reserved. Descant by Christopher Gower (b. 1939) © The Royal School of Church Music. Used by permission. First text: 'All creatures of our God and King' by William Henry Draper (1855–1933) based on St Francis. Second text: 'Ye watchers and ye holy ones' by Athelstan Riley (1858–1945) © Oxford University Press

# 46b LASST UNS ERFREUEN (in E♭)

All creatures of our God and King

*Ye watchers and ye holy ones*

Descant by Christopher Gower

Let all things their cre-a-tor bless,_ and wor-ship him. O____
*O friends, in glad-ness let us sing,_ su - per-nal an-thems, al -*

____ praise him,_ al - le - lu - ia! Praise the Fa - ther,
*- le - lu - ia,_ al - le - lu - ia! God the Fa - ther,*

praise the Son, Spi-rit,_Three in One:____ O___ praise him, O__
*God the Son, Spi-rit,_Three in One:____ Al - le - lu - ia, al-le-*

praise_him, Al-le - lu - ia, al-le - lu - ia, al-le - lu - - ia!
*-lu - ia, al-le - lu - ia, al-le - lu - ia, al-le - lu - - ia!*

*Lasst uns erfreuen* arr. by Ralph Vaughan Williams (1872–1958) from *The English Hymnal*. Reproduced by permission of Oxford University Press. All rights reserved. Descant by Christopher Gower (b. 1939) © The Royal School of Church Music. Used by permission. First text: 'All creatures of our God and King' by William Henry Draper (1855–1933) based on St Francis. Second text: 'Ye watchers and ye holy ones' by Athelstan Riley (1858–1945) © Oxford University Press

# 47a & b LAUDES DOMINI (in C and B♭)

When morning gilds the skies

Descant by Reginald Thatcher

47a in C

Be this, while life is mine,_ my can-ti-cle di - vine:__ may Je-sus Christ be praised.

Be this th'e-ter-nal song_through all the a-ges long:__may Je - sus_Christ be praised!
*through a-ges all a - long:__*

47b in B♭

Be this, while life is mine,_ my can-ti-cle di - vine:__ may Je-sus Christ be praised.

Be this th'e-ter-nal song_through all the a-ges long:__may Je - sus_Christ be praised!
*through a-ges all a - long:__*

*Laudes Domini* by Joseph Barnby (1838–96). Descant by Reginald Thatcher (1888–1957) © Oxford University Press
Text: 'When morning gilds the skies' translated by Edward Caswall (1814–78) from 19th-century German

# 48 LAUDS

There's a spirit in the air

Descant by John Wilson

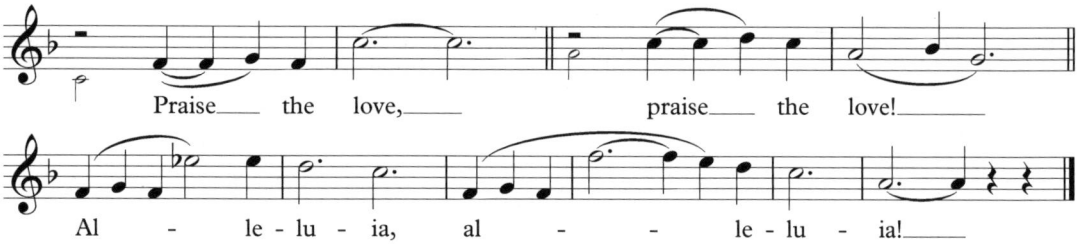


Hymn tune and descant by John Wilson (1905–92) © The Estate of John Wilson. Administered by Oxford University Press
Text: 'There's a spirit in the air' by Brian Wren (b. 1936) © 1969, 1995 Stainer & Bell Ltd, 23 Gruneisen Road, London N3 1DZ

# 49 LAUS DEO (REDHEAD No. 46)

Bright the vision that delighted

Descant from *Hymns Ancient & Modern Revised*
probably by Sydney H Nicholson

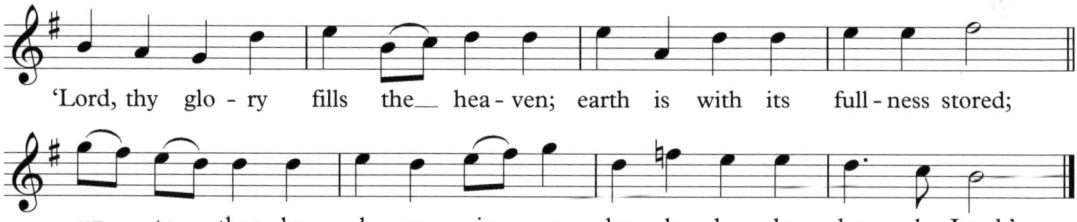


*Laus Deo* by Richard Redhead (1820–1901). Descant from *Hymns Ancient & Modern Revised* probably by Sydney H Nicholson (1875–1947) © Hymns Ancient & Modern Ltd. Used by permission.
Text: 'Bright the vision that delighted' by Richard Mant (1776–1848)

# 50a LOBE DEN HERREN (PRAXIS PIETATIS) (in F)

Praise to the Lord, the Almighty, the King of creation

Descant by Harrison Oxley

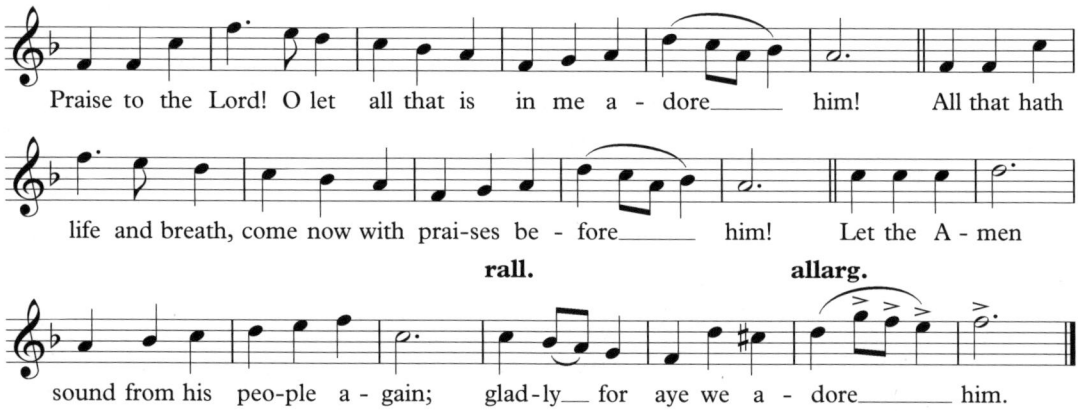


*Lobe den Herren*—17th-century German melody
Descant by Harrison Oxley (1933–2009) © 1988 The Royal School of Church Music. Used by permission
Text: 'Praise to the Lord, the Almighty' tr. by Catherine Winkworth (1827–78) from Joachim Neander (1650–80)

# 50b LOBE DEN HERREN (PRAXIS PIETATIS) (in G)

Praise to the Lord, the Almighty, the King of creation

Descant by Harrison Oxley

*Lobe den Herren*—17th-century German melody
Descant by Harrison Oxley (1933–2009) © 1988 The Royal School of Church Music. Used by permission
Text: 'Praise to the Lord, the Almighty' tr. by Catherine Winkworth (1827–78) from Joachim Neander (1650–80)

# 51 LORD OF THE YEARS

Lord, for the years your love has kept and guided

Descant by John Barnard

*Lord of the years* by Michael Baughen (b. 1930). Music © Michael Baughen / Jubilate Hymns; descant by John Barnard (b. 1948) © John Barnard / Jubilate Hymns. Administered by The Jubilate Group, 4 Thorne Park Road, Torquay TQ2 6RX <copyrightmanager@jubilate.co.uk> Used by permission
Text: 'Lord, for the years your love has kept and guided' by Timothy Dudley-Smith (b. 1926) © Timothy Dudley-Smith in Europe and Africa. © Hope Publishing Company in the United States of America and the rest of the world. Reproduced by permission of Oxford University Press. All rights reserved

# 52 LUCKINGTON

Let all the world in every corner sing

Descant by William Mathias

Let all the world in ev-ery cor-ner sing, my God and King.

The church with psalms must shout, no door can keep them out;

but a-bove all the heart must bear the long-est part.

**Allargando**

Let all the world in ev-ery cor-ner sing, my God and King.

*Luckington* by Basil Harwood (1859–1949) © The Estate of Basil Harwood
Descant by William Mathias (1934–92) from his anthem *Let all the world in every corner sing* © 1987 Oxford University Press
Text: 'Let all the world in every corner sing' by George Herbert (1593–1633)

# 53 LUX EOI

Alleluia, alleluia! Hearts to heaven and voices raise

Descant by Richard Lloyd

Al - le-lu - ia, al - le - lu - ia! Glo - ry be to God on high;

Al - le-lu - ia to the Sa-viour, who has gained the vic - to - ry;
*to the Fa - ther, and the Sa - viour,*

Al - le - lu - ia to the Spi - rit, fount of love and sanc - ti - ty:
*glo - ry to the Ho - ly Spi - rit,*

Al - le - lu - - ia! to the Tri - une Ma - je - sty.

*Lux eoi* by Arthur Sullivan (1842–1900)
Descant by Richard Lloyd (b. 1933) © 1990 Kevin Mayhew Ltd. Reproduced by permission; Licence Nr 217011/1
<www.kevinmayhew.com>
Text: 'Alleluia, alleluia! Hearts to heaven and voices raise' by Christopher Wordsworth (1807–85)

# 54a MACCABAEUS (in E♭)

Thine be the glory, risen, conquering Son

Descant by Malcolm Archer

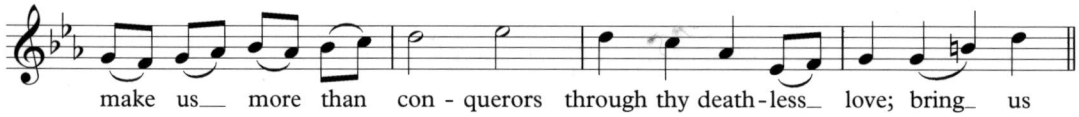

*Maccabaeus* by G F Handel (1685–1759). Descant by Malcolm Archer (b. 1952) © 1990 Kevin Mayhew Ltd.
Reproduced by permission; Licence Nr 217011/1 <www.kevinmayhew.com>
Text: 'Thine be the glory, risen, conquering Son' by Richard Hoyle (1875–1939) from Edmond Budry (1854–1932)

# 54b MACCABAEUS (in D)

Thine be the glory, risen, conquering Son

Descant by Malcolm Archer

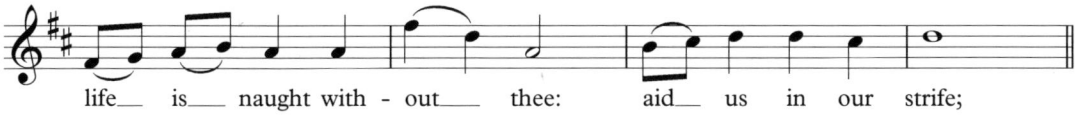

*Maccabaeus* by G F Handel (1685–1759). Descant by Malcolm Archer (b. 1952) © 1990 Kevin Mayhew Ltd.
Reproduced by permission; Licence Nr 217011/1 <www.kevinmayhew.com>
Text: 'Thine be the glory, risen, conquering Son' by Richard Hoyle (1875–1939) from Edmond Budry (1854–1932)

# 55a & b MELCOMBE (in E♭ and D)

New every morning is the love

Descant by Alan Gray

55a in E♭

55b in D

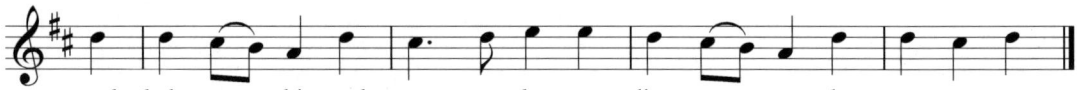


*Melcombe* by Samuel Webbe the elder (1740–1816)
Descant by Alan Gray (1855–1935)
Text: 'New every morning is the love' by John Keble (1792–1866)

# 56 MELITA

Eternal Father, strong to save

Descant by Alan Gray

*Melita* by John Bacchus Dykes (1823–76)
Descant by Alan Gray (1855–1935)
Text: 'Eternal Father, strong to save' by William Whiting (1825–78)

# 57a & b MENDELSSOHN (BETHLEHEM) (in F and G)

Hark! the herald-angels sing

Descant by David Willcocks

57a in F

Hail, the heaven-born Prince of Peace! Hail, the Sun of Right - eous- ness!

Light and life to all he brings, risen with heal - ing in his wings.

Mild he lays his glo - ry by, born that man no more may die,

born to raise the sons of earth, born to give them se - cond birth.

*ff*

*Hark! the he - rald - an - gels sing glo - ry to the new - born King.*

57b in G

Hail, the heaven-born Prince of Peace! Hail, the Sun of Right - eous- ness!

Light and life to all he brings, risen with heal - ing in his wings.

Mild he lays his glo - ry by, born that man no more may die,

born to raise the sons of earth, born to give them se - cond birth.

*ff*

*Hark! the he - rald - an - gels sing glo - ry to the new - born King.*

*Mendelssohn*—from a chorus in *Festgesang* by Felix Mendelssohn (1809–47)
Descant by David Willcocks (b. 1919) © 1961 Oxford University Press
Text: 'Hark! the herald-angels sing' by Charles Wesley (1707–88)

# 58a & b MERTON (in F and E)

Hark, a thrilling voice is sounding
*Jesus calls us: o'er the tumult*

Descant by Alan Gray

58a in F

58b in E




*Merton* by William Henry Monk (1823–89)
Descant by Alan Gray (1855–1935)
First text: 'Hark, a thrilling voice is sounding' translated by Edward Caswall (1814–78) from sixth-century Latin
Second text: 'Jesus calls us: o'er the tumult' by Cecil Frances Alexander (1818–95)

# 59 MILES LANE

All hail the power of Jesu's name

Descant by Alan Gray

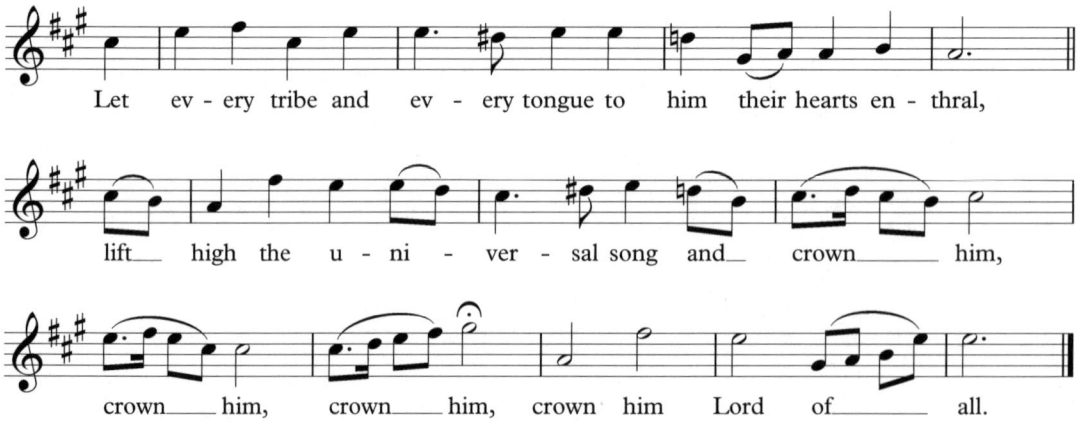


*Miles Lane* by William Shrubsole (?1760–1806)
Descant by Alan Gray (1855–1935)
Text: 'All hail the power of Jesu's name' by Edward Perronet (1721–92) and John Rippon (1751–1836)

# 60 MONKLAND

Let us, with a gladsome mind
*Praise, O praise our God and King*

Descant by John Wilson

*Monkland* by John Antes (1740–1811)
Descant by John Wilson (1905–92) © The Estate of John Wilson. Administered by Oxford University Press
First text: 'Let us, with a gladsome mind' by John Milton (1608–74)
Second text: 'Praise, O praise our God and King' by Henry Williams Baker (1821–77)

# 61 MONKS GATE

He who would valiant be
*Who would true valour see*

Descant by Cyril Winn

*Monks Gate*—English traditional melody collected, adapted, and arranged by Ralph Vaughan Williams (1872–1958) from *The English Hymnal*. Reproduced by permission of Oxford University Press. All rights reserved
Descant by Cyril Winn (1884–1973) © 1961 Oxford University Press
First text: 'He who would valiant be' by John Bunyan (1628–88) and Percy Dearmer (1867–1936)
Second text: 'Who would true valour see' by John Bunyan (1628–88)

# 62 MORNING HYMN

Awake, my soul, and with the sun

Descant by David Willcocks

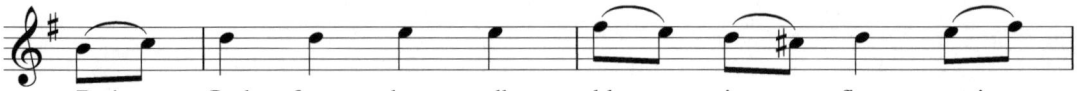

*Morning Hymn* by François H Barthélémon (1741–1808)
Descant by David Willcocks (b. 1919) © 2012 Oxford University Press
Text: 'Awake, my soul, and with the sun' by Thomas Ken (1637–1711)

# 63 MOSCOW

Thou whose almighty word

Descant by Alan Gray

*Moscow* by Felice de Giardini (1716–96)
Descant by Alan Gray (1855–1935)
Text: 'Thou whose almighty word' by John Marriott (1780–1825)

# 64 NEANDER (UNSER HERRSCHER)

Come, ye faithful, raise the anthem

Descant from *Hymns Ancient & Modern Revised*
probably by Sydney H Nicholson

Laud and ho - nour to the Fa - ther, laud and ho - nour to the Son,

laud and ho - nour to the Spi - rit, ev - er Three and ev - er One,

con - sub - stan - tial, co - e - ter - nal, while un - end - ing a - ges run.

*Neander* by Joachim Neander (1650–80)
Descant from *Hymns Ancient & Modern Revised* probably by Sydney H Nicholson (1875–1947) © Hymns Ancient & Modern Ltd. Used by permission
Text: 'Come, ye faithful, raise the anthem' — final verse by John Mason Neale (1818–66)

# 65 NICAEA

Holy, holy, holy! Lord God Almighty

Descant by James Vivian

Ho - ly, ho - ly! Lord God Al - might - y!

all thy works shall praise thy name in earth and sky and sea;

ho - ly, ho - ly, Lord God Al - might - y!

God in three per - sons, bless - ed Tri - ni - ty!

*Nicaea* by John Bacchus Dykes (1823–76)
Descant by James Vivian (b. 1974) © 2012 Oxford University Press
Text: 'Holy, holy, holy! Lord God Almighty' by Reginald Heber (1783–1826)

# 66 NOEL

It came upon the midnight clear

Descant by David Willcocks

*Noel*—English traditional melody adapted by Arthur Sullivan (1842–1900)
Descant by David Willcocks (b. 1919) © 1970 Oxford University Press
Text: 'It came upon the midnight clear' by Edmund Sears (1810–76)

# 67a NUN DANKET (in F)

Now thank we all our God

Descant by William H Harris

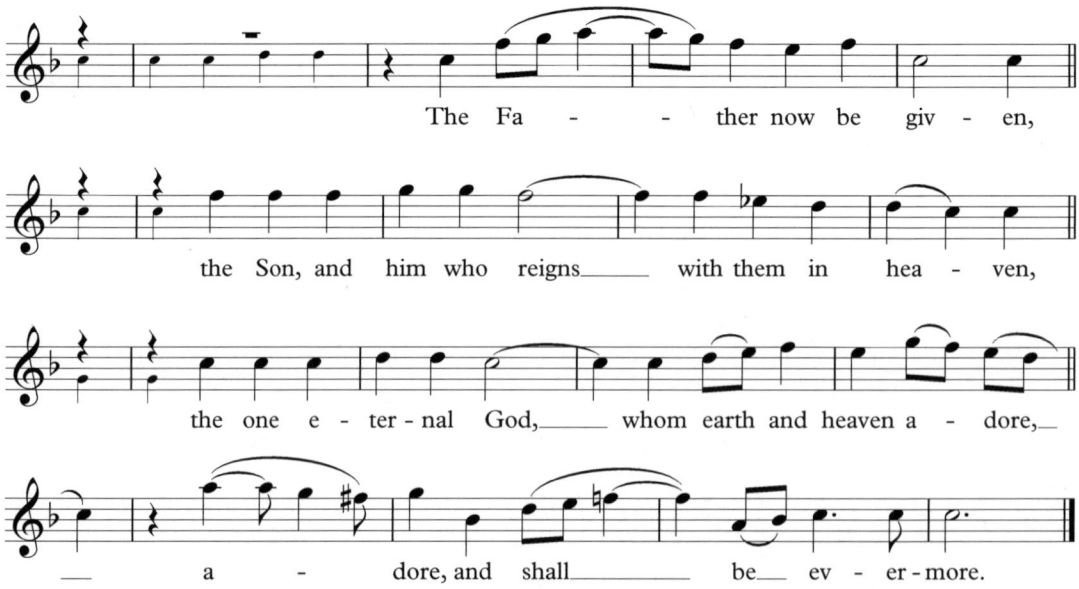


*Nun danket* probably by Johann Crüger (1598–1662)
Descant by William H Harris (1883–1973) © The Royal School of Church Music. Used by permission
Text: 'Now thank we all our God' translated by Catherine Winkworth (1827–78) from Martin Rinkart (1586–1649)

# 67b NUN DANKET (in E♭)

Now thank we all our God

Descant by William H Harris

*Nun danket* probably by Johann Crüger (1598–1662)
Descant by William H Harris (1883–1973) © The Royal School of Church Music. Used by permission
Text: 'Now thank we all our God' translated by Catherine Winkworth (1827–78) from Martin Rinkart (1586–1649)

# 68 ORIEL

To the name of our salvation

Descant by Alan Gray

*Oriel* from Caspar Ett's *Cantica Sacra* 1840
Descant by Alan Gray (1855–1935)
Text: 'To the name of our salvation' translated by John Mason Neale (1818–66) from 15th-century Latin

# 69 PRAISE, MY SOUL (LAUDA ANIMA)

Praise, my soul, the King of heaven

Descant by Alan Gray

*Praise, my soul* by John Goss (1800–80)
Descant by Alan Gray (1855–1935)
Text: 'Praise, my soul, the King of heaven' by Henry Francis Lyte (1793–1847)

# 70 PUER NOBIS NASCITUR

Come, thou Redeemer of the earth

Descant by John Scott

*Puer nobis nascitur*—medieval German carol melody adapted by Michael Praetorius (1571–1621)
Descant by John Scott (b. 1956) © 2001 Banks Music Publications. Reproduced by permission
Text: 'Come, thou Redeemer of the earth' translated by John Mason Neale (1818–66) from St Ambrose (*c.*340–97)

# 71 QUAM DILECTA

We love the place, O God

Descant by John Henderson

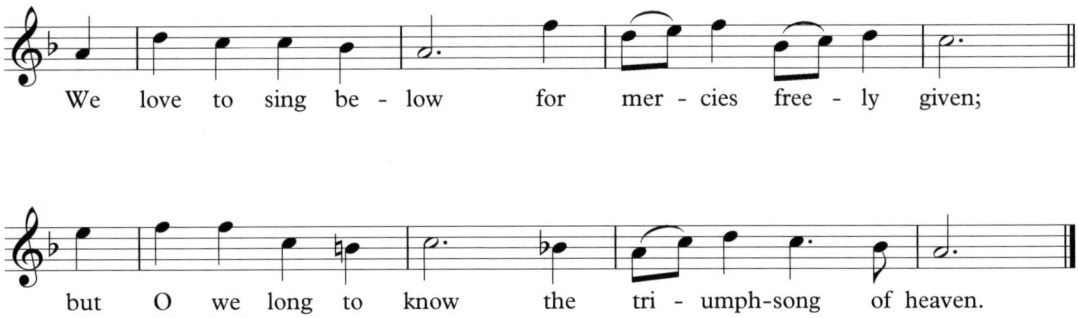


*Quam dilecta* by Henry Jenner (1820–98)
Descant by John Henderson (b. 1945) © 2012 Oxford University Press
Text: 'We love the place, O God'—final verses by Henry Williams Baker (1821–77)

# 72 REGENT SQUARE

Light's abode, celestial Salem

Descant by David Thorne

*Regent Square* by Henry Smart (1813–79)
Descant by David Thorne (b. 1950) © 2012 Oxford University Press
Text: 'Light's abode, celestial Salem' translated by John Mason Neale (1818–66) from 15th-century Latin

# 73 REPTON

Dear Lord and Father of mankind

Descant by John Scott

*Repton* by C Hubert H Parry (1848–1918)
Descant by John Scott (b. 1956) © 2001 Banks Music Publications. Reproduced by permission
Text: 'Dear Lord and Father of mankind' by John Greenleaf Whittier (1807–92)

# 74a RICHMOND (in F)

City of God, how broad and far

Descant by Edward Bairstow

*Richmond* by Thomas Haweis (1734–1820)
Descant by Edward Bairstow (1874–1946) © 1941 Oxford University Press
Text: 'City of God, how broad and far' by Samuel Johnson (1822–82)

# 74b RICHMOND (in G)

City of God, how broad and far

Descant by Edward Bairstow

*Richmond* by Thomas Haweis (1734–1820)
Descant by Edward Bairstow (1874–1946) © 1941 Oxford University Press
Text: 'City of God, how broad and far' by Samuel Johnson (1822–82)

# 75a & b ROCKINGHAM (in D and E♭)

When I survey the wondrous cross
*My God, and is thy table spread*

Composer of descant is unknown

75a in D

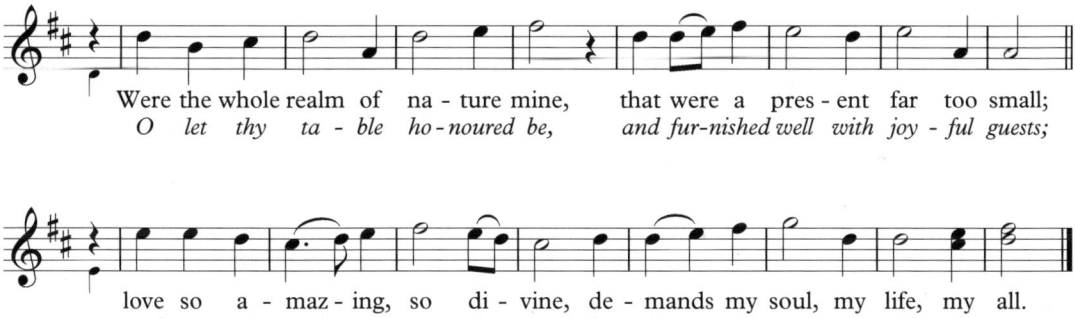


75b in E♭

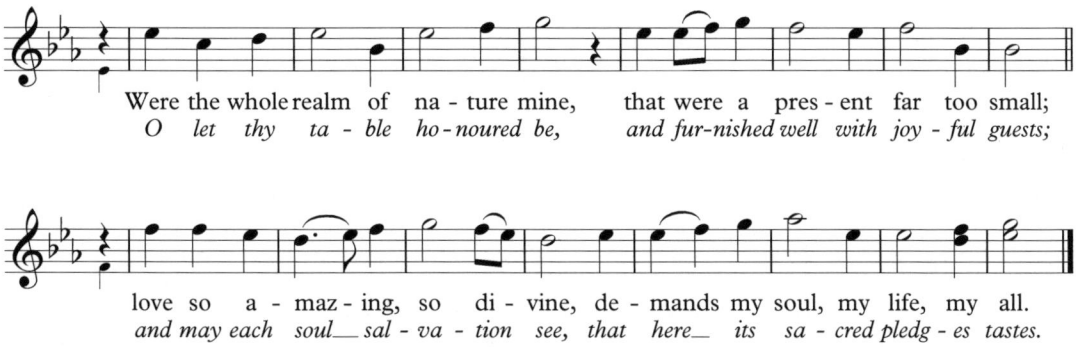


*Rockingham* adapted by Edward Miller (1735–1807)
First text: 'When I survey the wondrous cross' by Isaac Watts (1674–1748)
Second text: 'My God, and is thy table spread' by Philip Doddridge (1702–51)

# 76 SAFFRON WALDEN

Just as I am, without one plea

Descant by Simon Lole

Just as I am, of that free love

breadth, length, depth, height to prove, here for a sea - son,

then a - bove, O Lamb of God, I come.

*Saffron Walden* by Arthur H Brown (1830–1926)
Descant by Simon Lole (b. 1957) © 2012 Oxford University Press
Text: 'Just as I am, without one plea' by Charlotte Elliott (1789–1871)

# 77a & b ST ALBINUS (in C and B♭)

Jesus lives! thy terrors now

Descant by John Henderson

77a in C

Je-sus lives! to him the throne o-ver all the world is giv - en: may we go where

**molto allargando**

he is gone, rest and reign with him in hea - ven. Al - le - lu - ia!

77b in B♭

Je-sus lives! to him the throne o-ver all the world is giv - en: may we go where

**molto allargando**

he is gone, rest and reign with him in hea - ven. Al - le - lu - ia!

*St Albinus* by Henry J Gauntlett (1805–76)
Descant by John Henderson (b. 1945) © 2012 Oxford University Press
Text: 'Jesus lives! thy terrors now' translated by Frances E Cox (1812–97) from Christian Gellert (1715–69)

# 78 ST ANNE

O God, our help in ages past

Descant by John Scott

*St Anne* probably by William Croft (1678–1727)
Descant by John Scott (b. 1956) © 2012 Oxford University Press
Text: 'O God, our help in ages past' by Isaac Watts (1674–1748)

# 79a & b ST CLEMENT (in A♭ and G)

The day thou gavest, Lord, is ended

Descant by David Blackwell

79a in A♭

79b in G

*St Clement* by Clement C Scholefield (1839–1904)
Descant by David Blackwell (b. 1961) © 2012 Oxford University Press
Text: 'The day thou gavest, Lord, is ended' by John Ellerton (1826–93)

# 80 ST COLUMBA

The King of love my shepherd is

Descant by Donald Davison

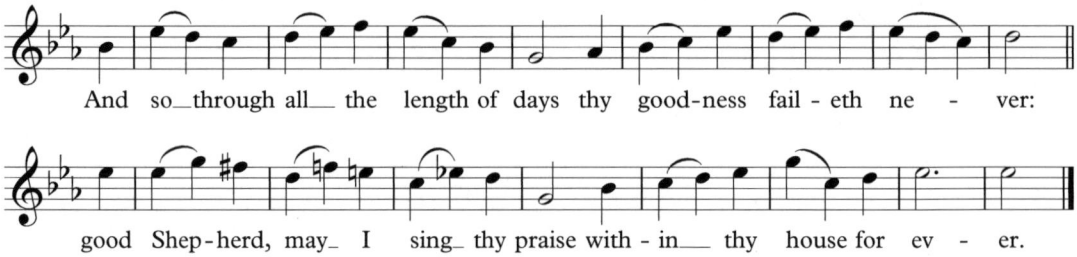


*St Columba*—Irish traditional melody
Descant by Donald Davison (b. 1937) © 2000 Oxford University Press
Text: 'The King of love my shepherd is' by Henry Williams Baker (1821–77)

# 81a & b ST DENIO (in A♭ and G)

Immortal, invisible, God only wise

Descant by Cyril Winn

81a in A♭

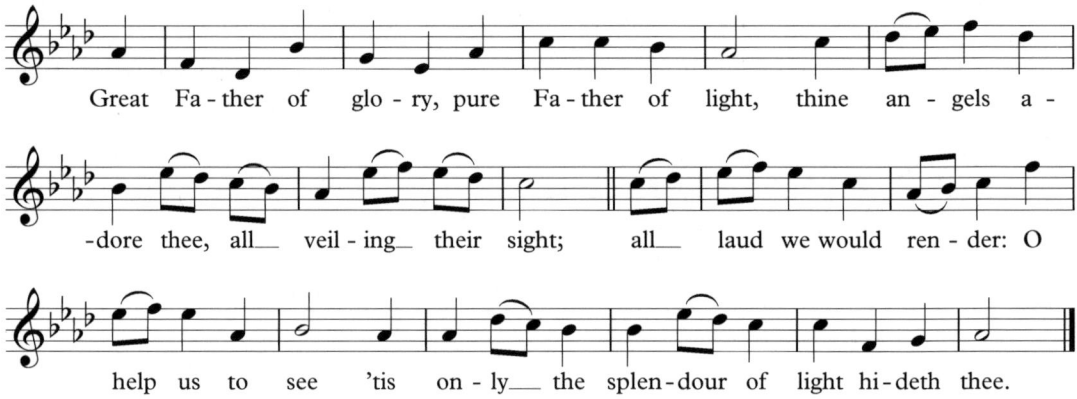


81b in G

*St Denio* adapted from a Welsh traditional melody
Descant by Cyril Winn (1884–1973) © 1961 Oxford University Press
Text: 'Immortal, invisible, God only wise' by W Chalmers Smith (1824–1908)

# 82 ST GEORGE'S WINDSOR

Come, ye thankful people, come

Descant by Robert Gower

Then, thou Church Tri - um - phant, come, raise the song of har - vest - home;
*E - ven so, Lord, quick - ly come, to thy fi - nal har - vest - home;*

all be safe - ly ga - thered in, free from sor - row, free from sin;
*ga - ther thou thy peo - ple in, free from sor - row, free from sin;*

come,
*come,*

come, raise the glo-rious har - vest - home!
*come, bid us sing thy har - vest - home!*

*St George's Windsor* by George J Elvey (1816–93)
Descant by Robert Gower (b. 1952) © 2012 Oxford University Press
Text: 'Come, ye thankful people, come' by Henry Alford (1810–71)

# 83 ST HELEN

Lord, enthroned in heavenly splendour

Descant by Christopher Gower

Life - im - part-ing heaven-ly man-na, strick-en rock with stream-ing side, heaven and

earth with loud ho - san - na wor-ship thee, the Lamb who died. Al -

- le - lu - ia, al - le - lu - ia, risen, a - scend - ed, glo - ri - fied!

*St Helen* by George C Martin (1844–1916)
Descant by Christopher Gower (b. 1939) © 1989 Kevin Mayhew Ltd. Reproduced by permission; Licence Nr 217011/1
<www.kevinmayhew.com>
Text: 'Lord, enthroned in heavenly splendour' by George H Bourne (1840–1925)

# 84 ST MAGNUS

The head that once was crowned with thorns

Descant by John Wilson

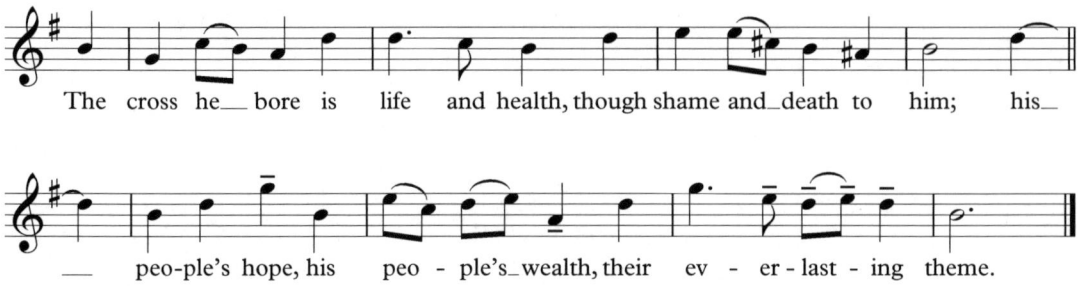


*St Magnus* probably by Jeremiah Clarke (*c.*1674–1707)
Descant by John Wilson (1905–92) © The Estate of John Wilson. Administered by Oxford University Press
Text: 'The head that once was crowned with thorns' by Thomas Kelly (1769–1855)

# 85 SEEK YE FIRST

Seek ye first the kingdom of God

Descant by William Llewellyn

Melody and words by Karen Lafferty (b. 1948)
© 1972 CCCM Music & Maranatha! Music / Universal Music (Print/Sync rights in the UK/Eire only by Small Stone Media BV, Holland). Administered by Song Solutions Daybreak <www.songsolutions.org>

# 86 SINE NOMINE

For all the saints who from their labours rest

Descant by Cyril Winn

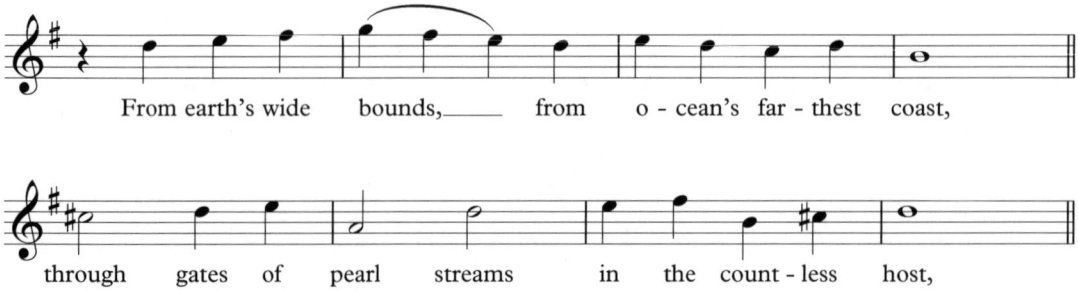


*Sine Nomine* by Ralph Vaughan Williams (1872–1958) from *The English Hymnal*. Reproduced by permission of Oxford University Press. All rights reserved.
Descant by Cyril Winn (1884–1973) © 1961 Oxford University Press.
Text: 'For all the saints who from their labours rest' by W Walsham How (1823–97)

## 87a & b SING HOSANNA (in E♭ and D)

Give me joy in my heart, keep me praising
Give me oil in my lamp, keep me burning

Traditional descant

87a in E♭

87b in D

Music and words from anonymous sources
© 2012 Oxford University Press

## 88a SLANE

Be thou my vision, O Lord of my heart

Descant by John Wilson

*Slane*—Irish traditional melody harmonized by Erik Routley (1917–82) © Oxford University Press
Descant by John Wilson (1905–92) © The Estate of John Wilson. Administered by Oxford University Press
Text: 'Be thou my vision, O Lord of my heart'—Irish, versified by Eleanor Hull (1860–1935) from Mary Byrne's translation

# 88b SLANE

Lord of all hopefulness, Lord of all joy

Descant by David Thorne

Lord of all gen - tle - ness, Lord of all calm,

whose voice is con - tent - ment, whose pres - ence is balm,

be there at our sleep - ing, and give us, we pray,

your peace in our hearts, Lord, at the end of the day.

*Slane*—Irish traditional melody harmonized by Erik Routley (1917–82) © Oxford University Press
Descant by David Thorne (b. 1950) © 2012 Oxford University Press
Text: 'Lord of all hopefulness, Lord of all joy' by Jan Struther (Joyce Placzek) (1901–53)

# 89 SONG 34 (ANGELS' SONG)

Forth in thy name, O Lord, I go

Descant by Donald Davison

For thee de - light-ful - ly em-ploy what-e'er thy boun-teous grace hath given,

and run my course with e - ven joy, and close-ly walk with thee to heaven.

Alternative opening rhythm

For thee de - light - ful-ly em-ploy

*Song 34* by Orlando Gibbons (1583–1625)
Descant by Donald Davison (b. 1937) © 2000 Oxford University Press
Text: 'Forth in thy name, O Lord, I go' by Charles Wesley (1707–88)

# 90a & b STUTTGART (in G and F)

Earth has many a noble city

*Come, thou long-expected Jesus*

Descant by Antony Baldwin

90a in G

Je - su, whom the_ Gen - tiles_ wor - shipped at thy glad_ E - pi - pha - ny,
*By thine own e - ter - nal_ Spi - rit,_ rule in all_ our hearts a - lone:*

un - to thee with God the_ Fa - ther and the Spi-rit glo - ry be.
*by thine all - suf - fi - cient_ me - rit, raise us to thy glo - rious throne.*

90b in F

Je - su, whom the_ Gen - tiles_ wor - shipped at thy glad_ E - pi - pha - ny,
*By thine own e - ter - nal_ Spi - rit,_ rule in all_ our hearts a - lone:*

un - to thee with God the_ Fa - ther and the Spi-rit glo - ry be.
*by thine all - suf - fi - cient_ me - rit, raise us to thy glo - rious throne.*

*Stuttgart* adapted from Witt's *Harmonia Sacra* 1715
Descant by Antony Baldwin (b. 1957) © 2000 Oxford University Press
First text: 'Earth has many a noble city' translated by Edward Caswall (1814–78) from Prudentius (348– *c.*413)
Second text: 'Come, thou long-expected Jesus' by Charles Wesley (1707–88)

# 91 THE SERVANT KING

From heaven you came, helpless babe

Descant by Ashley Grote

**Worshipfully**

So let us learn how to serve, and in our lives en-throne_

_ him; each o-ther's needs to pre - fer, for it is Christ we're serv - ing.

*This is our God,_ the Ser-vant King, he calls us now to fol-low him,*

*to bring our lives_ as an of-fer-ing of wor-ship to the Ser-vant King.*

Music and words by Graham Kendrick (b. 1950)
Descant by Ashley Grote (b. 1982)
© 1983 Thankyou Music / Administered by worshiptogether.com Songs, excluding UK & Europe, administered by kingswaysongs, a division of David C Cook <tym@kingsway.co.uk> Used by permission

# 92 THORNBURY

Thy hand, O God, has guided

Descant by David Willcocks

Thy mer - cy will not fail us, nor leave thy work un - done;

with thy right hand to help us, the vic - tory shall be won;

and then by men and an - gels, thy name shall be a - dored,

and this shall be their an - them: one church, one faith, one faith, one Lord.

*Thornbury* by Basil Harwood (1859–1949) © The Estate of Basil Harwood
Descant by David Willcocks (b. 1919) © 2012 Oxford University Press
Text: 'Thy hand, O God, has guided' by Edward H Plumptre (1821–91)

# 93a & b TRURO (in D and C)

Jesus shall reign where'er the sun

*Christ is alive! Let Christians sing*

Descant by John Wilson

93a in D

Let ev - ery crea - ture rise and bring pe - cu - liar ho - nours to our King;
*Christ is a - live, and comes to bring good news to this and ev - ery age,*

an-gels des-cend with songs a - gain, and earth re - peat the loud A - men.
*till earth and sky and o - cean ring with joy, with jus - tice, love, and praise.*

93b in C

Let ev - ery crea - ture rise and bring pe - cu - liar ho - nours to our King;
*Christ is a - live, and comes to bring good news to this and ev - ery age,*

an-gels des-cend with songs a - gain, and earth re - peat the loud A - men.
*till earth and sky and o - cean ring with joy, with jus - tice, love, and praise.*

*Truro*—melody from Thomas Williams's *Psalmodia Evangelica* 1789
Descant by John Wilson (1905–92) © The Estate of John Wilson. Administered by Oxford University Press
First text: 'Jesus shall reign where'er the sun' by Isaac Watts (1674–1748)
Second text: 'Christ is alive! Let Christians sing' by Brian Wren (b. 1936) © 1969, 1995 Stainer & Bell Ltd

# 94a VENI EMMANUEL (metrical version)

O come, O come, Emmanuel

Descant by Robert Gower

*Veni Emmanuel*—melody adapted by Thomas Helmore (1811–90)
Descant by Robert Gower (b. 1952) © 2012 Oxford University Press
Text: 'O come, O come, Emmanuel' translated by John Mason Neale (1818–66) from Latin Advent Antiphons

# 94b VENI EMMANUEL (plainchant version)

O come, O come, Emmanuel

Descant by Robert Gower

*Veni Emmanuel*—melody adapted by Thomas Helmore (1811–90)
Descant by Robert Gower (b. 1952) © 2012 Oxford University Press
Text: 'O come, O come, Emmanuel' translated by John Mason Neale (1818–66) from Latin Advent Antiphons

# 95a & b WAREHAM (in B♭ and A)

Jesus, where'er thy people meet
*Rejoice, O land, in God thy might*

Descant from *Hymns Ancient & Modern Revised*
by Sydney H Nicholson

95a in B♭

Lord, we are few, but thou art near; nor short thine arm, nor deaf_ thine ear;
*He shall for - give thy sins_ un - told: re - mem - ber thou his love_ of old;*

O rend the heavens, come quick-ly down, and make a thou-sand hearts thine own!
*walk in his way, his word a - dore, and keep_ his truth for ev - er - more.*

95b in A

Lord, we are few, but thou art near; nor short thine arm, nor deaf_ thine ear;
*He shall for - give thy sins_ un - told: re - mem - ber thou his love_ of old;*

O rend the heavens, come quick-ly down, and make a thou-sand hearts thine own!
*walk in his way, his word a - dore, and keep_ his truth for ev - er - more.*

*Wareham* by William Knapp (1698–1768)
Descant from *Hymns Ancient & Modern Revised* by Sydney H Nicholson (1875–1947) © Hymns Ancient & Modern Ltd. Used by permission.
First text: 'Jesus, where'er thy people meet' by William Cowper (1731–1800)
Second text: 'Rejoice, O land, in God thy might' by Robert Bridges (1844–1930)

# 96 WAS LEBET

O worship the Lord in the beauty of holiness

Descant by Donald Davison

O wor-ship the Lord in the beau - ty of ho - li-ness! Bow down be-

-fore him, his glo - ry___ pro - claim; with gold of o - be-dience, and

in - cense of low - li-ness, kneel and a - dore him: the Lord is his name!

*Was lebet*—melody from the *Rheinhardt MS* 1754
Descant by Donald Davison (b. 1937) © 2000 Oxford University Press
Text: 'O worship the Lord in the beauty of holiness' by John S B Monsell (1811–75)

# 97a & b WESTMINSTER ABBEY (in A♭ and G)

Blessed city, heavenly Salem
Christ is made the sure foundation

Descant by John Rutter

97a in A♭

*f*

Laud_ and ho - nour to the Fa - ther, laud and ho - nour

to___ the Son, laud_ and ho - nour___ to the Spi - rit,___ ev - er

*cresc.*

Three,_ and ev - er One, con - sub - stan - tial, co - e - ter - nal,

*ff* **Largamente**

while___ un - end - ing,_ un - end - ing,_ un - end-ing a - ges_ run.

97b in G

*f*

Laud_ and ho - nour to the Fa - ther, laud and ho - nour

to___ the Son, laud_ and ho - nour___ to the Spi - rit,___ ev - er

*cresc.*

Three,_ and ev - er One, con - sub - stan - tial, co - e - ter - nal,

*ff* **Largamente**

while___ un - end - ing,_ un - end - ing,_ un - end-ing a - ges_ run.

*Westminster Abbey* adap. Henry Purcell (1659–95)
Descant by John Rutter (b. 1945) © 2000 Collegium Music Publications.
Text: 'Blessed city, heavenly Salem' ('Christ is made the sure foundation') tr. by John Mason Neale (1818–66)

# 98 WINCHESTER NEW

On Jordan's bank the Baptist's cry
*Ride on, ride on in majesty*

Descant by Alan Gray

All praise, e - ter - nal Son, to thee whose
*Ride on, ride on in ma - jes - ty! In*

ad - vent sets thy peo - ple free, whom with the Fa - ther
*low - ly pomp ride on to die; bow thy meek head to*

we a - dore, and Ho - ly Ghost for ev - er - more.
*mor - tal pain, then take, O God, thy power, and reign.*

*Winchester New* adapted from *Musikalisches Hand-Buch* 1690
Descant by Alan Gray (1855–1935)
First text: 'On Jordan's bank the Baptist's cry' tr. by John Chandler (1806–76)
Second text: 'Ride on, ride on in majesty' by Henry H Milman (1791–1868)

# 99 WINCHESTER OLD

While shepherds watched their flocks by night

Descant by Alan Gray

'All glo - ry be to God on high, and to the earth be peace;

good - will hence-forth from heaven to men be - gin and ne - ver cease.'
(earth)

*Winchester Old* from Thomas Este's *Psalter* 1592
Descant by Alan Gray (1855–1935)
Text: 'While shepherds watched their flocks by night' by Nahum Tate (1652–1715)

# 100a WOODLANDS

'Lift up your hearts!' We lift them, Lord, to thee

Descant by Richard Lloyd

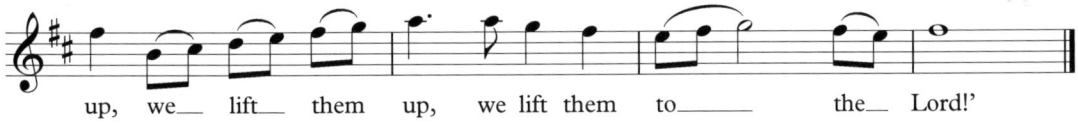


*Woodlands* by Walter Greatorex (1877–1949) © Oxford University Press
Descant by Richard Lloyd (b. 1933) © 1990 Kevin Mayhew Ltd. Reproduced by permission; Licence Nr 217011/1
<www.kevinmayhew.com>
Text: '"Lift up your hearts!" We lift them, Lord, to thee' by H Montagu Butler (1833–1918)

# 100b WOODLANDS

Tell out, my soul, the greatness of the Lord

Descant by Benjamin Lamb

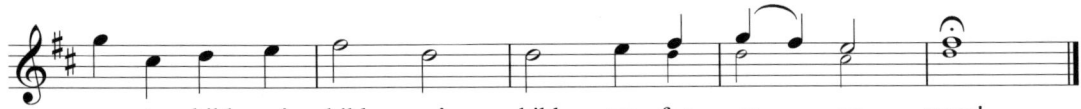


*Woodlands* by Walter Greatorex (1877–1949) © Oxford University Press
Descant by Benjamin Lamb (b. 1974) © 2012 Oxford University Press
Text: 'Tell out, my soul, the greatness of the Lord' by Timothy Dudley-Smith (b. 1926) © Timothy Dudley-Smith in Europe and Africa. © Hope Publishing Company in the United States of America and the rest of the world. Reproduced by permission of Oxford University Press. All rights reserved